WALKING
IN THE
SPIRIT

WALKING
IN THE
SPIRIT

HOW TO FULFILL THE ULTIMATE
PURPOSE OF CHRISTIANITY

PASTOR A.O. ASABOR

REDEMPTION
PRESS

Published by Redemption Press, PO Box 427, Enumclaw, WA 98022.

ISBN 13: 978-1-63232-454-2
Library of Congress Catalog Card Number: 2011925086

CONTENTS

CHAPTER 1

INTRODUCTION

THE SACRIFICIAL DEATH of Jesus for our sins brought the old creation to an end because everything in the old creation died in Him (see details in Chapter 4), while the coming of the Holy Spirit brought the reality of the new creation in Christ. Put in another way, the death of Jesus, by which the old is terminated, makes it possible for us to be part of the new creation through the new birth, while the Holy Spirit manifests the reality of the new birth in us. Without the Holy Spirit there will be neither new birth nor its manifestation because, as children of God, we are born of the Spirit (John 3:5–6) and required to be led by the Spirit (Romans 8:14). The problem is, many have accepted the new birth but have ignored or rejected the Holy Spirit. This is most pathetic especially in the case of those in the Pentecostal circle to whom the ministry of the Holy Spirit is supposed to be foundational belief. Failure to believe or accept the ministry of the Holy Spirit is the reason there is so much manifestation of the flesh in Christianity of today. This is the main reason why becoming like Jesus has remained a struggle for most Christians. In my first book, titled the *Ultimate Purpose of Christianity*, it was emphasized that the ultimate purpose of Christianity is to produce the likeness of God in man. It was also emphasized that the new birth, which is the means by which God

1

recreates us in His image that was distorted by sin at the garden of Eden, is the beginning of the process by which His likeness is reproduced in us. Unfortunately, many have taken the beginning of the process as an end in itself; that is, they assume that the process is already completed just because they have given their lives to Jesus or because they are born again. If that is correct, why then did the apostle Paul say,

> "Don't you realize that everyone who runs in a race runs to win, but only one runner gets the prize? Run like them, so that you can win. Everyone who enters an athletic contest goes into strict training. They do it to win a temporary crown, but we do it to win one that will be permanent. So I run—but not without a clear goal ahead of me. So I box—but not as if I were just shadow boxing, Rather, I toughen my body with punches and make it my slave so that I will not be disqualified after I have spread the Good News to others"?
>
> —1 Corinthians 9:24–27 GWT

The bottom line is that it is possible to be disqualified even after you have been actively involved in preaching the good news or laboring in the church. Don't let anyone fool you; Christianity is a process that begins with being born again, and as such being born again is not an end in itself but the compulsory or mandatory and unavoidable starting point. The real problem is that we have ignored God's method and have tried to establish our own just as the children of Israel ignored God's righteousness and tried to establish their own. "Brethren, my heart's desire and prayer to God for Israel is, that they might be saved. For I bear them record that they have a zeal of God, but not according to knowledge. For they being ignorant of God's righteousness, and going about to establish their own righteousness, have not submitted themselves unto the righteousness of God" (Romans 10:1–3). The sad part is that they were not only ignorant of God's righteousness but actually tried to establish their own righteousness, which they must have assumed was of God or acceptable to God. Today we are ignorantly falling into the same error. If we are going to fulfill the ultimate purpose of

Christianity, which is to become like Jesus, we must return back to God's plan and method. We can never become like Jesus or fulfill the ultimate purpose of Christianity until we acknowledge, accept, and allow the ministry of the Holy Spirit in our lives. God's method is very simple—be born again and become His child, recreated in His image; be led by the Spirit and mature to become a son in His likeness. "For as many as are led by the Spirit of God, they are the sons of God" (Romans 8:14). It is really very simple; only those who will allow themselves to be led by the Holy Spirit are the ones who will mature or grow to become sons of God. We are recreated in His image by being born again, but we become like Him by being led by the Holy Spirit. To be led by the Spirit is to walk in the Spirit. The difference between being led by the Holy Spirit and walking in the Spirit is simply the perspective you are viewing them from. Leading is what the Holy Spirit does, but walking in the Spirit is what we do as a result of the leading. Thus, being led by the Holy Spirit and walking in the Spirit are two sides of the same coin. We can also say that walking in the Spirit is what we do that gives effect to the leading of the Spirit in our lives. Leading is the role of the Holy Spirit while walking in the Spirit is our role. There can never be any issue with the role of the Holy Spirit, but there are a lot of issues with our walking in the Spirit, and this is the reason for this book. The opposite of walking in the Spirit is walking in the flesh, and if we fail to walk in the Spirit, we will walk in the flesh by default. As long as we are walking in the flesh, we cannot walk in the Spirit, and we will not be led by the Spirit, who usually does not force Himself on anyone. If we are going to become like Jesus, we must be led by the Spirit, meaning we must walk in the Spirit.

WALKING IN THE SPIRIT IS MANDATORY

Walking in the Spirit is not a matter of choice; it is mandatory. The Bible says, "There is therefore now no condemnation to them which are in Christ Jesus, who walk not after the flesh, but after the Spirit" (Romans 8:1). The question is, do you want to be free from condemnation? If your answer is yes, then you have no choice but to walk in the Spirit. It is only those who will stop walking in the flesh by walking in the Spirit who are not under condemnation. "This I say then, Walk in the Spirit, and ye shall not fulfill the lust of the flesh. For the flesh lusteth against the Spirit, and the Spirit against the flesh: and these are contrary the one to the other: so that ye cannot do the things that ye would. But if ye be led of the Spirit, ye are not under the law" (Galatians 5:16–18). You have been called to walk in the Spirit, and it is as you walk in the Spirit that you overcome the lust of the flesh. That is, the power of the flesh over you is broken as you walk in the Spirit. By the above Scripture it is also clear that it is as you are led by the Spirit that you are not under the law. That is, you are not under the law only when you allow the Holy Spirit to perform His role of leading you, which, if you respond to, becomes walking in the Spirit. The role of the Holy Spirit can be complete or effective only when you walk in the Spirit. Not being under the law implies that you are under grace, which means you are firmly planted in grace only when you are walking in the Spirit. That is to say, you experience, enjoy, and benefit from grace only when you walk in the Spirit or when you allow the leading of the Holy Spirit to manifest in your life. But the leading of the Holy Spirit will not manifest in your life automatically or by force. You allow its manifestation by walking in the Spirit. The Holy Spirit, through His leading, brings the resources of God into your life, but it is walking in the Spirit that puts them at your disposal. Which means sin, sicknesses/diseases, poverty, and all other works of the Devil cannot operate in your life when you are walking in the Spirit. Failure to walk in the Spirit is the root cause of most of the problems people are experiencing in church today. The Spirit and the flesh are contrary to each other, and the flesh will always manifest by default if you do not consciously walk in the Spirit. The problem of the church of today can be traced to people continuing to walk in the flesh though they have become children of God. To walk in the flesh is to allow your corrupt human nature to continue to lead or influence you. "Brothers and sisters, I couldn't talk to you as spiritual people but as people still influenced by your corrupt nature. You were infants in your faith in Christ. I gave you milk to drink. I didn't give you solid food because you weren't ready for it. Even now you aren't ready for it because you're still influenced by your corrupt nature. When you are jealous and quarrel among yourselves, aren't you influenced by your corrupt nature and living by human standards" (1 Corinthians 3:1–3 GWT). If this was an issue in the days of apostle Paul, such that he had to write to correct it, I wonder what we can say about the present time. There is too much of flesh in the Christianity of today, and you owe yourself the responsibility not to continue in it. One thing is sure: you cannot walk in the Spirit and in the flesh at the same time because they are contrary to each other. You are walking either in the Spirit or in the flesh. Walking in the Spirit one moment and the flesh the other cannot take you to the place God has prepared for you; only a continuous and consistent walk in the Spirit can take you there. Therefore the flesh must give way for the Spirit to thrive. "For when we were in the flesh, the motions of sins, which were by the law, did work in our members to bring forth fruit unto death. But now we are delivered from the law, that being dead wherein we were held; that we should serve in newness of spirit, and not in the oldness of the letter" (Romans 7:5–6). We all start in the flesh and move into the Spirit when we become children of God by the new birth. According to the above Scripture, as children of God, we are expected to serve in newness of spirit, which is possible only when we die to the flesh. "And they that are Christ's have crucified the flesh with the affections and lusts. If we live in the Spirit, let us also walk in the Spirit" (Galatians 5:24–25). This Scripture is saying that the proof or confirmation that you belong to Christ is the crucifixion of your flesh with the affections and lusts, which qualifies you to live and walk in the Spirit. Notice in the Scripture that there is a difference between living in the Spirit and walking in the Spirit. The fact that you live in the Spirit does not mean that you are walking in the Spirit. On the day you agreed to be born again, you were automatically born into the Spirit (1 Corinthians 12:12–13), but walking in the Spirit is not automatic; you have to walk in the Spirit by responding to or following the leading of the Holy Spirit. When you are born into the Spirit, your name is written in the Lamb's Book of Life, but maintaining your name in the book of life depends on how you walk in the Spirit. That is why walking in the Spirit must become our priority, and we must give it all our efforts and attention. The summary is that walking in the Spirit is mandatory for everyone who has become a child of God.

WALKING IN THE SPIRIT BRINGS PLEASURE TO GOD?

To walk in the Spirit is to allow all our actions and activities to proceed from and be executed by the Holy Spirit. That is why the Bible says, "For it is God which worketh in you both to will and to do of his good pleasure" (Philippians 2:13). Thus, walking in the Spirit makes our actions pleasing to God because they proceed from Him and are executed by His power. The truth is, the pleasure in what you do will always return to whoever originated and empowered such work or activity. To be specific, if the origin of any activity is the Devil, the pleasure will be his. In the same way, if the origin is a human being, the pleasure goes to the human being, and if it is you, the pleasure will also be yours. Thus, you can determine who gets the pleasure from the activities of your life by determining who empowered them. But the only person who really deserves the pleasure in what you do is God, if indeed you belong to Him. The Bible says, "He created you for His pleasure." Ask yourself, why would God create you if He does not desire or expect any pleasure from you? Just look at everything around you that is made by man. I do not know of anything that man has made that is not intended to bring him one form of pleasure or the other. The only reason man is putting so much effort into research today is to maximize the pleasure or satisfaction it provides. That is why vehicles are being continuously redesigned, so that they will not only meet the need of transportation but also provided comfort and pleasure at the same time. Understand; therefore, that God being your creator deserves the pleasure in all that you do, and don't forget that somebody will always get the pleasure in what you do anyway. That is why you must make deliberate effort to ensure that God is the One getting the pleasure in what you do. For God to get the pleasure in what you do, He must originate and execute such works or activities in you by His Holy Spirit.

God's simple plan is to make His will your will and then to execute that will in you. This is the only way that whatever is done in you can be satisfactory or acceptable and bring pleasure to Him. This is where many are missing it; they are just too anxious to do something for the Lord, but the truth is, if that thing does not originate from the Lord and is executed by the Lord, you have wasted your time and energy because such works will not give God any pleasure, nor will they survive the acid test of the kingdom of heaven. That is why Jesus warned that we can do nothing without Him "Abide in me, and I in you. As the branch cannot bear fruit of itself, except it abide in the vine; so neither can ye, except ye abide in me. I am the vine, ye are the branches: He that abideth in me, and I in him, the same beareth much fruit: for apart from me ye can do nothing" (John 15:4–5). The fact that you can do nothing does not mean that you will be idle or unable to carry out any activity; it simply means that without Jesus you cannot do anything that is of eternal value or that is acceptable to God. Worst still, it simply means that whatever you are doing without Jesus is worthless. Also see 1 Corinthians 3:11–15. "For other foundation can no man lay than that is laid, which is Jesus Christ. Now if any man build upon this foundation gold, silver, precious stones, wood, hay, stubble; Every man's work shall be made manifest: for the day shall declare it, because it shall be revealed by fire; and the fire shall try every man's work of what sort it is." After we are saved, everything we are doing will be tried by the holy fire of God at the end. For our work to withstand the fire of God, it must be according to His pattern. We need to be careful in whatever we are doing for the Lord, especially as the end is drawing nearer and nearer. The truth is that God is not expecting us to do anything for Him; rather He requires us to allow Him to work through us (Philippians 2:13). Put in another way, God wants to live through us such that our lives will be a manifestation of His workings in us. That is why the apostle Paul says, "I am crucified with Christ: nevertheless I live; yet not I, but Christ liveth in me: and the life which I now live in the flesh I live by the faith of the Son of God, who loved me, and gave himself for me. I do not frustrate the grace of God:

for if righteousness comes by the law, then Christ is dead in vain" (Galatians 2:20–21). As children of God we have been crucified with Christ, meaning that officially we no longer exist as we were but now exist only in union with Jesus. It is He who should now live in us. The Almighty, Omnipotent, and Omnipresent, who is the Creator of all things and to whom nothing is impossible, requires our consent to live and work in and through us. What an incredible privilege! When we allow God to live and work through us, we become His workmanship. "For we are his workmanship, created in Christ Jesus unto good works, which God hath before ordained that we should walk in them" (Ephesians 2:10). According to this Scripture, we are basically called to be God's workmanship. Unfortunately, whenever this passage of Scripture is read, the impression most people have is that we are to be God's tools. This is a grievous error because we are more than tools to God. There is a big difference between tools and workmanship. If all God wanted were tools, animals would have been sufficient for Him to achieve that purpose. The truth is that in creating man God desired more than tools; otherwise He would have made man like robots. His desire from the beginning is to have man as His workmanship. Understand that declaring us His workmanship is an abnormal use of the word because products are not usually described as workmanship but as evidence or a result of it. Note that man is the only created being that God has labeled workmanship, which means there is something unique that God has put in man. Let us illustrate this with the example of the robot. Though the robot is a product of man, in a way it is also man's workmanship, though in a limited sense. Once correctly programmed, the robot produces things as man himself would. Thus, the robot is not just a tool but an object that can exhibit workmanship. It is also the only product of man that has this capacity. The only difference between robot and man is that man has an independent will or capacity to make his own choices, whereas the robot, on the other hand, can do only what it has been programmed to do. The dictionary gives the meaning of *workmanship* as "formal skill in making things, especially in a way that makes them look good." If we apply this meaning to the above

Scripture, we will discover that we are actually recreated in Christ to be God's skill for doing things. The problem is that many of us are too humble to accept whom God says we are; I pray that God will open your eyes to behold this truth in Jesus's name. To make progress in the Christian life, we must be prepared to accept who or all that God says we are. Now, skill is actually the ability to do things and do them well. Thus, God has not just made His ability available to us; He has made us His skill for doing things. As God's skill we are required to use the ability He has made available to us to function or perform as Jesus did. "Verily, verily, I say unto you, He that believeth on me, the works that I do shall he do also; and greater works than these shall he do; because I go unto my Father" (John 14:12). Note that Jesus Himself was the one speaking, and He did not say the works will be done *through* you but *by* you. This is because we are to be workmanship, not tools. The power and wisdom for the work are not yours but in you by the Holy Spirit. Jesus is our example; whatever He did we ought to be able to do and even more. As God's skills nothing in the universe should be able to overcome us if we are utilizing the ability and functioning within the capacity God has made available to us. That is why the Bible says, "For everyone born of God overcomes the world. This is the victory that has overcome the world, even our faith" (1 John 5:4 NIV). If you are God's workmanship or functioning as the skill of God, there is no way the world can overcome you. In fact, the whole creation of God is expecting us to manifest as sons of God. "For the earnest expectation of the creature waiteth for the manifestation of the sons of God" (Romans 8:19). Note that sons of God speak of children of God maturing to become whom God has recreated them to be. Basically God has created us to become an extension of Him, which means God is enlarging His skill, and every one born of God has become an extension of God's skill. No wonder the Bible says, "But as it is written, Eye hath not seen, nor ear heard, neither have entered into the heart of man, the things which God hath prepared for them that love him. But God hath revealed them unto us by his Spirit: for the Spirit searcheth all things, yea, the deep things of God. For what man knoweth the things of a man, save the spirit of man which is in him? even so the things of God knoweth no man, but the Spirit of God" (1 Corinthians 2:9–11). We will understand this better in eternity. I don't want to digress too much, but I want you to understand that God has great plans for your life, and you must not waste the opportunity. You will agree with me that workmanship, skill, or ability cannot apply itself to work. That is why God has put His Spirit in you, but for the Spirit to function, you must agree and consciously yield yourself to Him; this is what walking in the Spirit is all about. You can function as God's workmanship only when you live and walk in the Spirit. That is, you cannot manifest or function as God's workmanship when you are still walking in the flesh.

It is sad that many, in an attempt to please the Lord, are actually laboring in the flesh. We must understand that God is interested not only in seeing work done through us but also in who does the work, whether it is the flesh or the Spirit. That is why God says "it is not by might or by power, but by my Spirit" (Zechariah 4:6). There is nothing that is done in the flesh that can ever please God. "Because the carnal mind is enmity against God: for it is not subject to the law of God, neither indeed can be. So then they that are in the flesh cannot please God" (Romans 8:7–8). Thus, walking in the flesh will always amount to offering strange fire before the Lord. Remember the case of Nadab and Abihu in Leviticus 10:1–2. "And Nadab and Abihu, the sons of Aaron, took either of them his censer, and put fire therein, and put incense thereon, and offered strange fire before the LORD, which he commanded them not. And there went out fire from the LORD, and devoured them, and they died before the LORD." Nadab and Abihu did what came to their minds instead of what God commanded, and they paid dearly with their lives. I am certain that Nadab and Abihu, if given the chance, would have argued that they were rendering service to God by offering the incense. Actually, there was nothing wrong with the incense, but in their state of drunkenness they thought any fire was OK. What they didn't realize at that point was that not all fire was acceptable to God. This should be a warning to us because the only fire that is acceptable to God is the fire of the Holy Ghost. Also note that there was another fire readily available to them. What is the fire/power behind what you are doing for the Lord? Now, when I say "what you are doing," I am not referring to pastors or ministers only; if you are a Christian, everything you are doing is for the Lord. "And whatsoever ye do in word or deed, do all in the name of the Lord Jesus, giving thanks to God and the Father by him" (Colossians 3:17). Also see 1 Corinthians 6:19–20. "What? know ye not that your body is the temple of the Holy Ghost which is in you, which ye have of God, and ye are not your own? For ye are bought with a price: therefore glorify God in your body, and in your spirit, which are God's." As a Christian everything you are doing must glorify God, and to glorify God means that it must be done only by the fire/power of God. Any other fire/power will be a strange fire.

Let's also see the example of Uzzah, who tried to help the ark of God when the oxen carrying it stumbled and also paid dearly with His life. "And David and all the house of Israel played before the LORD on all manner of instruments made of fir wood, even on harps, and on psalteries, and on timbrels, and on cornets, and on cymbals. And when they came to Nachon's threshingfloor, Uzzah put forth his hand to the ark of God, and took hold of it; for the oxen shook it. And the anger of the LORD was kindled against Uzzah; and God smote him there for his error; and there he died by the ark of God" (2 Samuel 6:5–7). God's anger was kindled against Uzzah because he responded to a spiritual matter in the flesh. Thus, strange fire also connotes the power of the flesh. These two examples show clearly that to labor for the Lord by any other power or the power of the flesh will always amount to offering strange fire before the Lord because you will be guilty of attempting to do the work of the Lord without the Lord of the work. That is why the Bible says, "Then he answered and spake unto me, saying, This is the word of the LORD unto Zerubbabel, saying, Not by might, nor by power, but by my spirit, saith the LORD of hosts" (Zechariah 4:6).

CHAPTER 2

LAYING PROPER FOUNDATION FOR WALKING IN THE SPIRIT

IN THIS CHAPTER, we shall establish the proper foundation for walking in the Spirit. This has become necessary because some basic spiritual issues that form the foundation for walking in the Spirit have been greatly misunderstood and are being misapplied. We can qualify these issues by grouping them as issues that encourage or support trying to do spiritual things in the flesh, as we have seen above. One such issue is the way obedience is being understood and applied in Christianity, which actually encourages or pushes people to work in the flesh. This wrong application of obedience is basically responsible for the crippled growth we are seeing in the life of many Christians today. Any attempt to please God in the flesh will always end in a struggle that will not produce the required result. To lay a proper foundation that will enable us to walk in the Spirit without struggling, there is a need to understand and put the issue of obedience in proper perspective.

OBEDIENCE

As children of God, we have become sons of obedience, but the issue of obedience, if not properly understood, can lead us back into bondage. In fact, it has already led many into bondage. We have been called into a life that demands complete obedience to God but not by our own effort or power. Complete obedience is the key factor in the discipleship process that will produce the likeness of God in us, but God knows that none of us can satisfy this important requirement. As a result, by His mercy He made provision for the requirement to be satisfied on our behalf. "For as by one man's disobedience many were made sinners, so by the obedience of one shall many be made righteous" (Romans 5:19). Just as we were made disobedient by the disobedience of Adam through the natural birth, so also we are made obedient by the obedience of Jesus through spiritual rebirth, and this is one of the reasons why we must be born again to begin the Christian race. Jesus did not only die to secure forgiveness for us, but by His obedience we are made obedient or righteous when we are born again or when we experience the new birth. *We must understand that we are not made righteous by our obedience but by the obedience of Christ.* The word *righteous* simply means doing what is right according to God's standard. We can say that by the obedience of Jesus we have been made a people who have the capacity to do what is right or a people who conform to the will of God. This was accomplished by the sacrifice of Jesus, by which we were made perfect. "By the which will we are sanctified through the offering of the body of Jesus Christ once for all. And every priest standeth daily ministering and offering oftentimes the same sacrifices, which can never take away sins: But this man, after he had offered one sacrifice for sins for ever, sat down on the right hand of God; from henceforth expecting till his enemies be made his footstool. For by one offering he hath perfected for ever them that are sanctified" (Hebrews 10:10–14). Note the last sentence, which says, "He hath perfected for ever them that are sanctified", which means it is completed. It was accomplished and given to us as a gift, which is why the righteousness of God, which is our perfection, is a gift. However, this perfection or righteousness is available only to those that are sanctified. Note that it doesn't say those who have been sanctified but those who are sanctified, meaning those who are in a continuous state of sanctification. "Elect according to the foreknowledge of God the Father, through sanctification of the Spirit, unto obedience and sprinkling of the blood of Jesus Christ: Grace unto you, and peace, be multiplied" (1 Peter 1:2). As a child of God you are one of God's elect, and the election is through sanctification, which leads to obedience and the sprinkling of the blood of Jesus. These are not your actions but the work of the Holy Spirit. In fact, let's see the above Scripture in *The Message* (MSG) translation. "God the Father has his eye on each of you, and has determined by the work of the Spirit to keep you obedient through the sacrifice of Jesus. May everything good from God be yours!" (1 Peter 1:2 MSG). We are kept obedient by the work of the Holy Spirit through the sacrifice of Jesus. We can say that sanctification, which is a work of the Spirit, leads, first and foremost, to obedience. Thus, allowing the Holy Spirit to carry out the work of sanctification in you will enable you to live a life of true obedience without any struggle. However, we need to understand that though sanctification is the work of the Holy Spirit, it is predicated on what Jesus has already done for us, referred to as His sacrifice. "For he hath made him to be sin for us, who knew no sin; that we might be made the righteousness of God in him" (2 Corinthians 5:21). We have been made righteous, but there is a condition—"in Him." As long as we are in Him, we are righteous, a people who conform to the will of God. By this gift of righteousness God has taken care of the issue of disobedience. Therefore our responsibility is not to try to be obedient but to manifest the obedience, which is the product of the righteousness or perfection that has been freely made available to us in Christ. Thus, you are to believe and be made obedient, and the proof of your faith is the obedience that manifests. Unfortunately, most Christians today now practice a mixture of faith and obedience in the flesh, which is totally unacceptable to God. We can boldly say that the free gift of righteousness is the complete solution to sin or disobedience. Therefore, for righteousness to be complete, it must provide a complete solution to the issue of sin. This is where many in Christianity have been made to believe half-truths; if your righteousness does not provide complete or total solution to sin, it is not of God. Sin is in three forms (usually referred to as the trio of sin); it is a person, a nature, and an action. To effectively take care of sin in its three forms, the righteousness of God must also be in the three forms, namely a person, a nature, and an action. The person of righteousness must replace the person of sin, and the nature of righteousness must replace the nature of sin before you can ever manifest the action of righteousness, which will prevent the action of sin from manifesting. Without the action of righteousness you may not earn any reward at the end. This shall not be your portion in Jesus's name. Let's examine the person, nature, and action of sin/righteousness a little further:

The Person of Sin: The person of sin is the Devil; that is why the Bible always refer to him as the spirit at work in those who are disobedient. "And you hath he quickened, who were dead in trespasses and sins; wherein in time past ye walked according to the course of this world, according to the prince of the power of the air, the spirit that now worketh in the children of disobedience" (Ephesians 2:1–2). Which means disobedience to God is a product of the working of the Devil, who is the prince of the power of the air. Note that it says, "The spirit that now worketh in the children of disobedience"; that is, if you are disobedient, it is this spirit that is actually at work in you. Meaning people are actually empowered to be disobedient by the Devil. That is why Jesus referred to the Devil as the father of those that were disobedient among the children of Israel. "Ye are of your father the devil, and the lusts of your father ye will do. He was a murderer from the beginning, and abode not in the truth, because there is no truth in him. When he speaketh a lie, he speaketh of his own: for he is a liar, and the father of it" (John 8:44). Remember that at the garden of Eden there was no sin until the Devil showed up. Thus, the Devil is the person of sin and the father of all who sin. "He that committeth sin is of the devil; for the devil sinneth from the beginning. For this purpose the Son of God was manifested, that he might destroy the works of the devil. Whosoever is born of God doth not commit sin; for his seed remaineth in him: and he cannot sin, because he is born of God. In this the children of God are manifest, and the children of the devil: whosoever doeth not righteousness is not of God, neither he that loveth not his brother" (1 John 3:8–10).

The Nature of Sin: Sin is also a nature, and the nature of sin is that part of you from where all sin is manifest. Every sin actually originates from the person of sin, but sins manifest through your nature. Thus, the person of sin always operates through the nature of sin, thereby transferring the responsibility of sin to you. The nature of sin is sometimes referred to as "the flesh" in some translations, while others refer to it as "the sinful nature" or "the carnal mind", but whether you call it "the flesh", "the sinful nature", "the carnal mind", or "the nature of sin", they all refer to the same thing. It is the part of you that is contrary to the Spirit of God which sets you at enmity with God. It is an obstacle to proper relationship with God. "For they that are after the flesh do mind the things of the flesh; but they that are after the Spirit the things of the Spirit. For to be carnally minded is death; but to be spiritually minded is life and peace. Because the carnal mind is enmity against God: for it is not subject to the law of God, neither indeed can be. So then they that are in the flesh cannot please God" (Romans 8:5–8). We can define the sinful nature as the inherent characteristics of our being that owe their source to the person of sin. For us to be free from sin, this nature of sin must be dealt with by what the Bible refers to as "spiritual circumcision". "In whom also ye are circumcised with the circumcision made without hands, in putting off the body of the sins of the flesh by the circumcision of Christ" (Colossians 2:11).

Sin as an Action: Finally, sin is also an action. This is the aspect of sin that is visible to or impacts others. It can simply be defined as those activities that result from the nature of sin, which the Bible refers to as the works of the flesh. "Now the works of the flesh are manifest, which are these; adultery, fornication, uncleanness, lasciviousness, idolatry, witchcraft, hatred, variance, emulations, wrath, strife, seditions, heresies, envying, murders, drunkenness, reveling, and such like: of the which I tell you before, as I have also told you in time past, that they which do such things shall not inherit the kingdom of God" (Galatians 5:19–21). All of these activities, whose list is not really exhaustive, are just symptoms, evidence that something more serious is wrong within the person. To illustrate this, let's use fornication as an example: the act of fornication is simply a symptom indicating that there is a person and nature of fornication inside. Fornication like all other sin will usually pass through a thought process before resulting in the action. The thought process is usually a communication between the person and the nature of sin in you. The action of sin can never happen until that thought process concludes in favor of the sin. For example, if during the thought process one decides against the sin, especially through the intervention of the person of righteousness, the action of fornication will not occur. Once the person and nature of sin are in agreement, the action of sin is empowered, and stopping it will be difficult. That is why I refer to the action of sin as mere symptom. Unfortunately most Christians are busy struggling with the symptoms and ignoring the real problem, which is the person and nature of sin. You can never really overcome sin and walk in the righteousness of God until you deal with the person and the nature of sin by replacing them with the person and nature of righteousness.

The Person of Righteousness: The person of righteousness is God Himself. When I use the word *God* here, I am referring to the Father, the Son, and the Holy Ghost, that is, the Godhead. Thus, the person of righteousness is the Godhead. However, Jesus, being the express image of the Godhead, is the one who manifests or reveals this righteousness of the Godhead to the creatures. "God, who at sundry times and in divers manners spake in time past unto the fathers by the prophets, hath in these last days spoken unto us by his Son, whom he hath appointed heir of all things, by whom also he made the worlds; **who being the brightness of His glory, and the express image of his person,** and upholding all things by the word of his power, when he had by himself purged our sins, sat down on the right hand of the Majesty on high" (Hebrews 1:1–3, emphasis added). Note that the image of His person in this Scripture refers to the image of the person of the Godhead, of which Jesus is a part. I am explaining this because people often read the above Scripture as if Jesus is a junior or a lesser God who has been sent

18

on an errand to the world. Don't ever forget that Jesus is Himself God, John 1:1–3 says, "In the beginning was the Word, and the Word was with God, and the Word was God. The same was in the beginning with God. All things were made by him; and without him was not any thing made that was made." And verse 14 says, "And the Word was made flesh, and dwelt among us, (and we beheld his glory, the glory as of the only begotten of the Father,) full of grace and truth". Jesus must never be seen as if He is junior in the Godhead just because He is called the Son. In fact, the Bible actually says that He is equal with God. "Have the same attitude that Christ Jesus had. Although he was in the form of God and equal with God, he did not take advantage of this equality. Instead, he emptied himself by taking on the form of a servant, by becoming like other humans, by having a human appearance. He humbled himself by becoming obedient to the point of death, death on a cross" (Phil 2:5–8 GWT). The fact that Jesus humbled Himself and emptied Himself to take the form of a servant when He came into the earth does not make Him less God. I needed to explain this so that we will not mix up the functions of Jesus as a member of the Godhead with His person in the Godhead. It is His function in the Godhead that brings Him out as the person of righteousness to God's creatures, and any creature who does not have Him can never manifest the righteousness of God. "And if Christ be in you, the body is dead because of sin; but the Spirit is life because of righteousness" (Romans 8:10). His indwelling you is the starting point of the righteousness of God in your life. Note from this Scripture that it is possible for your spirit to be made righteous because of the indwelling of Jesus while your body continues in sin. This is where many Christians encounter problems; they think that once they have Jesus, their bodies should automatically function in righteousness. I usually call this a half-truth, and that is why we must understand the role of the person, the nature, and the action of righteousness in our manifesting the righteousness of God that is credited to us when we become God's children. We can therefore boldly say that Jesus is the person of righteousness who must indwell us to position us for the righteousness of God.

Let me emphasize that without the indwelling of Jesus, no one can ever achieve the righteousness of God. That is why the Bible says Jesus has become our righteousness. "But of him are ye in Christ Jesus, who of God is made unto us wisdom, and righteousness, and sanctification, and redemption" (1 Corinthians 1:30). The Bible also says, "For Christ is the end of the law for righteousness to everyone that believeth" (Romans 10:4). Let us not misunderstand these Scriptures by thinking that our righteousness is complete just because we have Jesus indwelling us. The indwelling of Jesus is the beginning; we must add the nature and action of righteousness to complete the process of manifesting the righteousness of God.

The Nature of Righteousness: Like sin, righteousness is also a nature. Before we came to Christ, our nature was the flesh which was developed, right from the day we were born into this world, through our association with the world and the influence of the Devil and his host of darkness. However, when we give our lives to Jesus, God expects us to become partakers of the divine nature, which is the nature of righteousness. "Whereby are given unto us exceeding great and precious promises: that by these ye might be partakers of the divine nature, having escaped the corruption that is in the world through lust" (2 Peter 1:4). The divine nature is also known as the new man. God expects us to willingly do away with the old nature and put on the new one, which has been recreated in righteousness and true holiness. "And be renewed in the spirit of your mind; and that ye put on the new man, which after God is created in righteousness and true holiness" (Ephesians 4:23–24). If you are truly born again, there is a new you that has been created in righteousness and true holiness, which you can put on only by faith. Remember that God creates only by His word; thus your nature of righteousness has been spoken into existence, but you receive when you hear the word and believe. That is, we receive the nature of righteousness by believing whatever God says to us. Every word God speaks to you has capacity to impact righteousness to your nature. "For with the heart man believeth unto righteousness; and with the mouth confession is made unto salvation" (Romans 10:10). We shall deal with these issues in detail in the future, but for the purpose of this study I want you to understand and appreciate the need to develop your nature of righteousness as a replacement for the nature of sin. The person of righteousness, Jesus, can be received, but the nature of righteousness can be developed only through a transformation process that is a product of a consistent relationship with the person of righteousness. That is why Romans 12:2 says, "And be not conformed to this world: but be ye transformed by the renewing of your mind, that ye may prove what is that good, and acceptable, and perfect, will of God". Thus, the nature of righteousness is a product of a transformation resulting from the renewal of your mind. It is also important to note that there is no time when you will not have a nature because everything in life proceeds from your nature. As a result you are either operating from the nature of sin or from the nature of righteousness. Thus, any area of life where you have not developed the nature of righteousness, the nature of sin applies, and the nature that applies determines the person who rules in such areas of your life.

Righteousness as an Action: Righteousness is not complete until it manifests in our actions. We can say that the righteousness of God is a process that begins with our acceptance of Jesus Christ, who is the person of righteousness, which leads to the progressive replacement of the nature of sin with the nature of righteousness before the action of righteousness can manifest. Because the righteousness of God is primarily a person, we must first submit to Him, which implies our rejection of the person of sin before we can ever manifest righteousness. "For they being ignorant of God's righteousness, and going about to establish their own righteousness, have not submitted themselves unto the righteousness of God" (Romans 10:3). Note that the error of the children of Israel, according to this Scripture, was failure to submit to the righteousness of God, and today we are falling into the same error. That is why we are admonished to "awake to righteousness, and sin not; for some have not the knowledge of God: I speak this to your shame" (1 Corinthians 15:34). To be awake to righteousness is to sin not. If sin is still holding you captive in any area of life, it is probably because you have not yet submitted to the righteousness of God in that area of your life. "If ye know that he is righteous, ye know that every one that doeth righteousness is born of him" (1 John 2:29). It is everyone that doeth, not everyone that has righteousness that is born of God. Which means the proof that you are really born of God is your actions of righteousness. "Little children, let no man deceive you: he that doeth righteousness is righteous, even as he is righteous" (1 John 3:7). I cannot emphasize this enough, but you must be a doer of righteousness to qualify to be called a child of God. You cannot be a child of God and act like the Devil. "In this the children of God are manifest, and the children of the devil: whosoever doeth not righteousness is not of God, neither he that loveth not his brother" (1 John 3:10). Note that this Scripture was not written for unbelievers but for us who have become children of God and it was written as a warning so that we do not assume that we can continue in sin and remain children of God. Now, don't misunderstand me; the action of righteousness is not the same as works of righteousness. Works of righteousness refer to good works that do not have their foundation in the person and nature of righteousness. It is work that is accomplished purely by human effort, which is totally unacceptable to God. The action of righteousness, on the other hand, is a product of the process of God's righteousness, and it manifests when both the person and the nature of righteousness are in you. Your job is to bear it as fruit, which is why the Bible admonishes us to be full of the fruit of righteousness. "Being filled with the fruits of righteousness, which are by Jesus Christ, unto the glory and praise of God" (Philippians 1:11). Thus, the action of righteousness is not works but fruit, which the Lord by His Spirit produces in us.

> "But ye are not in the flesh, but in the Spirit, if so be that the Spirit of God dwell in you. Now if any man has not the Spirit of Christ, he is none of his. And if Christ be in you, the body is dead because of sin; but the Spirit is life because of righteousness. But if the Spirit of him that raised up Jesus from the dead dwell in you, he that raised up Christ from the dead shall also quicken your mortal bodies by his Spirit that dwelleth in you. Therefore,

brethren, we are debtors, not to the flesh, to live after the ..
For if ye live after the flesh, ye shall die: but if ye through the
Spirit do mortify the deeds of the body, ye shall live."
—Romans 8:9–13

If you continue to live according to the flesh, you should expect
nothing other than death no matter how long you have been born
again. The truth is that the Spirit that raised Jesus from the dead dwells
in us for the purpose of enabling us to overcome sin. From the above
Scripture, as a Christian you have the responsibility to mortify or put
to death the deeds of your body through the Spirit so that the action
of righteousness can manifest. In conclusion you need the person,
nature, and action of righteousness to manifest the righteousness of
God, which is the complete obedience expected of us.

COMPLETE OBEDIENCE

As we have seen, complete obedience occurs only when righteousness replaces sin at the three levels of its manifestation, that
is, as a person, nature, and action, which is possible only as we
walk in the Spirit. That is why the Bible says the righteousness of
the law is fulfilled in those who will stop walking in the flesh by
walking in the Spirit. "That the righteousness of the law might be
fulfilled in us, who walk not after the flesh, but after the Spirit"
(Romans 8:4). Thus, walking in the Spirit is the key to manifesting
the complete obedience of Jesus. Complete obedience for us is a
product of walking in the Spirit, and the manifestation of this
complete obedience is called the fruit of the Spirit. "But the fruit
of the Spirit is love, joy, peace, longsuffering, gentleness, goodness,
faith, meekness, temperance: against such there is no law"
(Galatians 5:22). What God expects from us is to allow the Holy
Spirit to bear fruit in us, and this is possible only as we walk in the
Spirit. The principle of fruit bearing is die and bear fruit. "Verily,
verily, I say unto you, Except a corn of wheat fall into the ground
and die, it abideth alone: but if it die, it bringeth forth much fruit"
(John 12:24). Fruit bearing does not come as a result of obeying
some rules and regulations, but fruit bearing fulfills all the

requirements of obedience. For example, I can in obedience give to the poor all that I have without loving the poor, but if I truly love the poor, as a result of the manifestation of the fruit of the Spirit in my life, I will naturally, gladly, and joyfully provide for them. "If I give all I possess to the poor and surrender my body to the flames, but have not love, I gain nothing" (1 Corinthians 13:3 NIV). Let's also try to understand this from the example of walking in the flesh. When we were in the flesh, we were not led by some set of rules and regulations; rather the flesh made us carry out its desires, or we conformed to the will of the flesh. In any area where the flesh made demands on us, it also provided the ability to perform. As a result we didn't have to struggle to satisfy our flesh. Our actions proceeded from the flesh, and the flesh enabled us to perform them. The body was not a problem because it will always perform according to the signal it receives from our inner being. This is the reason why the flesh finds it very easy to reign in us. Walking in the Spirit is very much similar. "And I will put my spirit within you, and cause you to walk in my statutes, and ye shall keep my judgments, and do them" (Ezekiel 36:27). Note the words "I will…cause you to." God's plan is that He will put His Spirit in us, and the signals that determine our actions will originate from the Spirit through the renewed mind. The strength and the ability to execute will come not from us but from the Holy Spirit. In this way your body will perform whatever signal it receives without any struggle. Now, when we were in the flesh, we had no choice because it was the only way of life we knew. We were born with the flesh, which the world, the Devil and his agents helped to shape and fuel for their purpose. As a result, we walked in the flesh automatically. Walking in the Spirit, on the other hand, is not automatic though it is mandatory. In fact, just as we had to choose to be born into the spirit, so also we need to choose to walk in the Spirit. That is, we have to choose to allow the Holy Spirit to work in us both to will and to do of His good pleasure. However, the moment we choose to walk in the Spirit and actually begin to, fruit bearing will automatically follow. Note that we walk while the Holy Spirit works. That is why the issue of obedience, if not properly understood and applied, will hinder us from making the right choices, and we will end up struggling to perform spiritual activities in the flesh; what an uphill task. One of the reasons for wrong application of obedience is the error of viewing flesh as all evil. Don't misunderstand me; in the sight of God the flesh is all evil, but don't forget that the flesh is a product of the Tree of Knowledge of Good and Evil. When Adam and evil sinned in the garden of Eden by eating from the Tree of Knowledge of Good and Evil, the result was the flesh. You can read that in Genesis 3. The issue is that the flesh is capable of some measure of good; that is why we have some unbelievers who are referred to as good. Such people actually perform works of righteousness in the flesh, but such works of righteousness are like filthy rags before God. "But we are all as an unclean thing, and all our righteousnesses are as filthy rags; and we all do fade as a leaf; and our iniquities, like the wind, have taken us away" (Isaiah 64:6). Such people have trained their flesh to perform some measure of good works without the person and nature of righteousness; however, in the face of serious opposition and pressure such training usually crumbles. Such training usually succeeds only in suppressing the works of the flesh. Not recognizing that the flesh is capable of some measure of good is a serious problem. The flesh is capable of the fruit of the Holy Spirit to the extent that it has been trained though such manifestation is usually a counterfeit. No matter the amount of good works the flesh is trained to perform, it will remain in opposition to God. Have you not noticed that, in most cases, it is easier to win a wicked man than to convert a seemingly good man? The more of God's principles man can obey in the flesh, the more He will resist God. That is why in the sight of God, there is nothing more unclean than the flesh; it is the mother of all sin. My major concern is that the way the issue of obedience is being treated and applied is encouraging Christians to walk in the flesh rather than in the Spirit, and the more they seem to be succeeding, the more they unconsciously resist God. In fact, struggling to obey is a hindrance to walking in the Spirit. Struggling is an indication that you are rejecting the gift of righteousness. When faced with death, the flesh does not mind being trained to perform some acts of obedience in order to be allowed to live, but the flesh can never be trained for complete obedience. In any given matter, the flesh can be obedient only to a certain measure. The flesh can never be trained to achieve perfection. That is why God's solution for the issue of the flesh is death; to be free of the flesh, your flesh must die (Colossians 2:11–12). Thus, it is no longer an issue of training yourself in obedience; what you need is crucifixion or mortifying or putting your flesh to death. Another reason why the issue of obedience is misunderstood and misapplied is because we have not learned to separate God's dealings with Israel from God's dealings with the church. In God's dealing with Israel, righteousness was by obedience to the totality of the law. "For as many as are of the works of the law are under the curse: for it is written, Cursed is every one that continueth not in all things which are written in the book of the law to do them" (Galatians 3:10). Obeying all aspects of the law was a condition for righteousness and living. "And the law is not of faith: but, the man that doeth them shall live in them" (Galatians 3:12). Whereas to the Christian, righteousness is purely a gift to be received and manifested by faith. "For if by one man's offence death reigned by one; much more they which receive abundance of grace and of the gift of righteousness shall reign in life by one, Jesus Christ" (Romans 5:17). Note that it is the gift of righteousness that enables us to reign in life with Christ. It is not a struggle but a reign. "But now the righteousness of God without the law is manifested, being witnessed by the law and the prophets" (Romans 3:21). Let's understand the fact that in the case of Israel, God was relating with them in the flesh (in the natural), and that is why it was necessary to give them rules and regulations for entering into God's presence and for relating with one another. It was an attempt to deal with the evil in the flesh to produce a good person, but it didn't work because the flesh is never capable of complete obedience. In fact, God's verdict after dealing with Israel in the flesh was "For all have sinned, and come short of the glory of God" (Romans 3:23). And the conclusion was "For God has bound all men over to disobedience so that he may have mercy on them all" (Romans 11:32 NIV).

The implication of this Scripture is that if you are a human being you will be naturally disobedient to God until you contact the mercy of God through salvation in Christ. Any salvation that does not take care of disobedience is incomplete. Obedience to prescribed laws is the ultimate requirement if the flesh is to be trained or made usable "But we know that the law is good, if a man use it lawfully; Knowing this, that the law is not made for a righteous man, but for the lawless and disobedient, for the ungodly and for sinners, for unholy and profane, for murderers of fathers and murderers of mothers, for manslayers" (1 Timothy 1:8–9 NIV). Note that laws are never made for the righteous but for the lawless. The flesh is the root of lawlessness in mankind. Just as God has no plans to change the world because the world is reserved for destruction. "But the day of the Lord will come as a thief in the night; in the which the heavens shall pass away with a great noise, and the elements shall melt with fervent heat, the earth also and the works that are therein shall be burned up" (2 Peter 3:10). In the same way, God has no plans to train the flesh to become righteous but to destroy it and replace it with the new man. The problem of mankind is the flesh. It is the flesh that makes a man a son of disobedience, and God's solution for disobedience is circumcision of the flesh "In whom also ye are circumcised with the circumcision made without hands, in putting off the body of the sins of the flesh by the circumcision of Christ" (Colossians 2:11).

The flesh has no place in the scheme of God. In God's plan, the old creation must give way completely to the new. "Therefore if any man be in Christ, he is a new creature: old things are passed away; behold all things are become new" (2 Corinthians 5:17). The old man must go before the new man can appear. Any man in whom the flesh has been put to death is a man in whom sin no longer has power to reign. He is a man who has overcome sin, and that is the man who cannot sin according to 1 John 3:6–9. "Whosoever abideth in him sinneth not: whosoever sinneth hath not seen him, neither known him. Little children, let no man deceive you: he that doeth righteousness is righteous, even as he is righteous. He that committeth sin is of the devil; for the devil sinneth from the beginning. For this purpose the Son of God was manifested, that he might destroy the works of the devil. Whosoever is born of God doth not commit sin; for his seed remaineth in him: and he cannot sin, because he is born of God." Therefore, let us understand that Jesus did not come to manage the works of the devil in our lives but to destroy them. The flesh, which is a product of the Devil and the world, must die before the new you can appear. Please do yourself a favor: stop trying to train your flesh to perform acts of righteousness because it will not work, and all such acts of righteousness are as filthy rags before the Lord. They will hinder your walk in the Spirit and deny you all the privileges that are available to those who walk in the Spirit. *Our obedience does not produce righteousness, but we are obedient because we have been made righteous as we receive the person of righteousness and develop the nature of righteousness.* Without first learning to walk in the Spirit, all efforts at obedience are useless. It is time for our emphasis to shift from obedience to walking in the Spirit, where our priority should be. Show me a man who walks in the Spirit, and I will show you a man who is obedient, in whom the life of Christ is freely manifested. Is this an attempt to undermine obedience? God forbid! It is to put obedience in its proper place. Failure to put obedience in its proper place will lead to attempts to obey in the flesh, which amount to obeying without believing, and that is dangerous. This, unfortunately, is the state of many in the church today.

We cannot conclude this part on obedience without looking at the Scriptures that talk about the obedience of Jesus, which have been greatly misunderstood. "Who in the days of his flesh, when he had offered up prayers and supplications with strong crying and tears unto him that was able to save him from death, and was heard in that he feared; though he were a Son, yet learned he obedience by the things which he suffered" (Hebrews 5:7–8). It is true that Jesus learned obedience through the things He suffered, but obedience to whom? I am certain that the apostle Paul was not implying that Jesus struggled to obey God or that He learned to obey God through the things He suffered because Jesus never had any problem obeying God. Otherwise He would not qualify as the perfect Lamb for the sacrifice that brings salvation to mankind. "But with the precious blood of Christ, as of a lamb without blemish and without spot" (1 Peter 1:19). Though Jesus came as man, He lived and walked only and always in the Spirit. We can say with all confidence that He never walked in the flesh (corrupt human nature); that is why He could declare confidently that the prince of this world had nothing in Him. "Hereafter I will not talk much with you: for the prince of this world cometh, and hath nothing in me. But that the world may know that I love the Father; and as the Father gave me commandment, even so I do. Arise, let us go hence" (John 14:30–31). Jesus always did as the Father commanded by the Spirit, and this is what qualified Him as the perfect Lamb without blemish and without spot. He was led by the Spirit all through His life here on earth. However, Jesus needed to learn obedience to man. In the days of His flesh, when man did not recognize Him as God, He had cause to submit to the authority of man from time to time. One clear example is the incident between Him and His earthly parents at the age of twelve. Let us see the summary of that story: "When his parents saw him, they were shocked. His mother asked him, 'Son, why have you done this to us? Your father and I have been worried sick looking for you!' Jesus said to them, 'Why were you looking for me? Didn't you realize that I had to be in my Father's house?' But they didn't understand what he meant. Then he returned with them to Nazareth and was obedient to them. His mother treasured all these things in her heart" Luke 2:48–51 (GWT). Through this and other similar experiences Jesus learned to obey His earthly parents. That is not to say that He was disobedient to them at any time but that He learned to adjust Himself to their misunderstanding of His person, mission, and actions. Also remember the story of Jesus turning water to wine.

> "And both Jesus was called, and his disciples, to the marriage. And when they wanted wine, the mother of Jesus saith unto him, They have no wine. Jesus saith unto her, Woman, what have I to do with thee? mine hour is not yet come. His mother saith unto the servants, Whatsoever he saith unto you, do it. And there were set there six waterpots of stone, after the manner of the purifying

of the Jews, containing two or three firkins apiece. Jesus saith unto them, Fill the waterpots with water. And they filled them up to the brim. And he saith unto them, Draw out now, and bear unto the governor of the feast."

—John 2:2–8

Though He declared that His time had not yet come, He had to do the wish of His earthly mother. We can say, therefore, that the obedience Jesus learned through the things He suffered bother around areas where He had to submit to man in order to fulfill His ministry. Other examples are His arrest, torture, and crucifixion, in all of which He had to submit to man.

Now, let us go back to Hebrews 5:7–9. "Who in the days of his flesh, when he had offered up prayers and supplications with strong crying and tears unto him that was able to save him from death, and was heard in that he feared; though he were a Son, yet learned he obedience by the things which he suffered; and being made perfect, he became the author of eternal salvation unto all them that obey him." We need to further understand that the prayers and supplications with strong crying and tears that Jesus offered were not because He was afraid of death or because He wished to disobey God. The Bible records that He prayed, "Let this cup pass over me, not my will but thy will be done," which means He knew exactly what the will of God was, and He was ready to do that will, but He needed to align Himself with the source of His ability, which is the Holy Spirit. Once again I believe that the problem here was not obedience to God but submission to mankind, His own creation, who was to perform the act that would put Him to death.

Walking in the Spirit is the real example Jesus left for us to follow. All He did in words and actions were done in and by the Spirit. God wants to lead us to the point where we will live and walk entirely in the Spirit because in the Spirit there is life and outside the Spirit there is death.

CHAPTER 3

WHY WALK IN THE SPIRIT?

IN CHAPTERS 1 and 2, we laid the foundation for a smooth walk in the Spirit. We emphasized that true or complete obedience, which is a vital requirement for a successful Christian life, is a product of the Spirit, which manifests as we walk in the Spirit. We cannot earn or achieve obedience on our own. Any obedience that is not a product of the Spirit is a product of the flesh, and such obedience is totally unacceptable to God. In fact, such obedience is an abomination before God. The good news is that just as we were made disobedient by natural birth, we have also been made obedient by the spiritual birth, and this obedience manifests as we walk in the Spirit. Just as disobedience was the result of walking in the flesh, obedience is also the result of walking in the Spirit. This is the reason why the new birth is a must for everyone who really wants to walk with God. As declared in Chapter 2, any salvation that does not address or provide a solution for the issue of your disobedience to God is incomplete. The aim of the cross was not only to appease God for our sins but also to provide a final solution to the issue of disobedience. "But this man, after he had offered one sacrifice for sins forever, sat down on the right hand of God; from henceforth expecting till his enemies be made his footstool. For by one offering he hath perfected for ever them that are sanctified"

(Hebrews 10:12–14). This is what makes the difference between the new and the old covenant. In the old covenant, man was given an opportunity to earn or gain life through obedience to the law, but he failed because none could keep the whole of the law. In the new covenant, the root of disobedience, the flesh, was identified and destroyed. The flesh is the source of all sin; and the only way we can have true victory over sin is to eliminate the flesh. God's solution for the problem of the flesh is death, and this is what Jesus accomplished for us on the cross. The issue of obedience was emphasized because when wrongly applied, it is a major hindrance to walking in the Spirit. "That as sin hath reigned unto death, even so might grace reign through righteousness unto eternal life by Jesus Christ our Lord" (Romans 5:21). Note that the grace of God, which the Bible says has appeared to all men (Titus 2:11), reigns only through righteousness. Righteousness here is referring to the righteousness of God, which we become when we are born again. "For he hath made him to be sin for us, who knew no sin; that we might be made the righteousness of God in him" (2 Corinthians 5:21). At the new birth we are made the righteousness of God, and without this righteousness the grace of God cannot reign in our lives. Wherever grace is not allowed to reign, sin will continue to reign. If sin is still reigning in any area of your life, it simply means that grace has not been allowed to reign in that area, and that is because you have not exercised enough faith in the free gift of righteousness that was made available to you at the new birth. The obedience required to enable grace to reign in our lives is in the gift of righteousness. Let me emphasize again that because God knew that none of us can ever achieve the obedience or righteousness required for His grace to reign in our lives, He made us obedient by the obedience of Jesus (Romans 5:19). As we proceed to look at why we must walk in the Spirit, let us understand and become conscious of the fact that we have been made obedient by the obedience of Jesus and that this obedience is fully manifested only as we walk in the Spirit. Walking in the Spirit is the place where grace is evidently put to use in every activity.

WHY WALK IN THE SPIRIT?

I have always believed that when we know why God wants us to do something, it will be a lot easier for us to believe and submit to Him in doing that thing. If Adam and Eve had understood why God commanded them not to eat of the Tree of Knowledge of Good and Evil, they would probably have been in a better position to resist the Devil or would have put in more effort to resist him. Seeing things from God's perspective will enable us to agree with Him quickly and act accordingly. If we are going to succeed in our walk with God, we must learn to think as He thinks to enable us to act in accordance with His will. Understanding why God demands that we walk in the Spirit will help us respond properly. The following are some of the reasons why we must walk in the Spirit:

1. **God is Spirit.**

God is Spirit, and our contact and relationship with Him are possible only in the Spirit. "But the hour cometh, and now is, when the true worshippers shall worship the Father in spirit and in truth: for the Father seeketh such to worship him. God is a Spirit: and they that worship him must worship him in spirit and in truth" (John 4:23–24). Jesus said the true worshipper must worship God in spirit and in truth. We have no choice in this matter; if we are going to be listed among the true worshippers, we must learn to worship Him in spirit and in truth. Note that the word Jesus used is *must* and also note that Jesus referred to those who worship in spirit and in truth as true worshippers, meaning that anyone whose worship is not in spirit and in truth is a false worshipper. It doesn't matter how much effort such a person may put into that kind of worship; as long as it is not in the Spirit, it will be a false and unacceptable worship. In fact, such worship does not come before God at all. Man is spirit, soul, and, body; and it is only in our regenerated spirit that we can worship God acceptably. We are worshipping either in the spirit or in the flesh.

2. You are born of the Spirit.

"But as many as received him, to them gave he power to become the sons of God, even to them that believe on his name: Which were born, not of blood, nor of the will of the flesh, nor of the will of man, but of God" (John 1:12–13). To be born again is to be born of God Himself, and to be born of God is to become a spirit being just like God. "Jesus answered, Verily, verily, I say unto thee, Except a man be born of water and of the Spirit, he cannot enter into the kingdom of God. That which is born of the flesh is flesh; and that which is born of the Spirit is spirit" (John 3:5–6). You are a spirit being. Did you hear that? I am not sure, so let me repeat it. I said, "You are a spirit being." I pray that you will receive this truth deep within your heart. If you are born again, you have been born of the Spirit, and you are a spirit being, but you still dwell in a physical body, which will eventually give way to the spiritual body you will receive at the return of Christ.

> "But some man will say, How are the dead raised up? and with what body do they come? Thou fool, that which thou sowest is not quickened, except it die: And that which thou sowest, thou sowest not that body that shall be, but bare grain, it may chance of wheat, or of some other grain: But God giveth it a body as it hath pleased him, and to every seed his own body. All flesh is not the same flesh: but there is one kind of flesh of men, another flesh of beasts, another of fishes, and another of birds. There are also celestial bodies, and bodies terrestrial: but the glory of the celestial is one, and the glory of the terrestrial is another. There is one glory of the sun, and another glory of the moon, and another glory of the stars: for one star differeth from another star in glory. So also is the resurrection of the dead. It is sown in corruption; it is raised in incorruption: It is sown in dishonour; it is raised in glory: it is sown in weakness; it is raised in power: It is sown a natural body; it is raised a spiritual body. There is a natural body, and there is a spiritual body."
>
> —1 Corinthians 15:35–44

At the resurrection we shall receive a spiritual body that will make us complete spiritual beings. In fact, the Bible says that we shall become exactly like Jesus when we see Him. "Beloved, now are we the sons of God, and it doth not yet appear what we shall be: but we know that, when he shall appear, we shall be like him; for we shall see him as he is" (1 John 3:2). Right now, the real you is a spirit that can manifest and express himself or herself only as you walk in the Spirit. Walking anywhere else apart from the Spirit amounts to caging the real you, preventing the manifestation of God's promises in your life and causing you to think that God has not done what He promised.

3. You are one spirit with Christ.

"But he who is united to the Lord becomes one spirit with him" (1 Corinthians 6:17 RSV). From the day you accepted Jesus as your Lord and Savior, you were united with Him and became one spirit with Him. You actually became a member of His body. "For we are members of his body, of his flesh, and of his bones; for this cause shall a man leave his father and mother, and shall be joined unto his wife, and they two shall be one flesh. This is a great mystery: but I speak concerning Christ and the church" (Ephesians 5:30–32). You will agree with me that it is impossible to be a member of His body and not be one spirit with Him. Just as God made Eve from what He took out of Adam, so also at salvation God makes us from what He has taken from Jesus. As a result, we have become one spirit with Him, a member of His own body. The new you is not only a spirit being but also one spirit with Christ; that is, you and Christ have become one spirit. You have become an extension of Christ such that He is no longer complete without you. "Which is his body, the fulness of him that filleth all in all" (Ephesians 1:23). The new you, which is now one spirit with Christ, will be effective only as you walk in His Spirit—the Holy Spirit. Note that we are not just to walk in the spirit but in the Holy Spirit. Are you beginning to appreciate why walking in the Spirit is a must for everyone who has become a child of God?

4. The Spirit is our new habitat.

"But ye are not in the flesh, but in the Spirit, if so be that the Spirit of God dwell in you. Now if any man has not the Spirit of Christ, he is none of his" (Romans 8:9). If you are born again, you have not only become a spirit being and one spirit with Christ, but your environment has also changed. You are now in the Spirit; that is, you now live in the Spirit. "If we live in the Spirit, let us also walk in the Spirit" (Galatians 5:25). Walking in the Spirit is possible and required of us only because we already live in the Spirit. The Spirit became our new environment at the new birth. The real you now lives in the Spirit. For a better understanding, let's return to Genesis. In Genesis, everything God created was created from and for a particular environment.

> "And God said, Let the waters bring forth abundantly the moving creature that hath life, and fowl that may fly above the earth in the open firmament of heaven. And God created great whales, and every living creature that moveth, which the waters brought forth abundantly, after their kind, and every winged fowl after his kind: and God saw that it was good. And God blessed them, saying, Be fruitful, and multiply, and fill the waters in the seas, and let fowl multiply in the earth. And the evening and the morning were the fifth day. And God said, Let the earth bring forth the living creature after his kind, cattle, and creeping thing, and beast of the earth after his kind: and it was so. And God made the beast of the earth after his kind, and cattle after their kind, and everything that creepeth upon the earth after his kind: and God saw that it was good."
>
> —Genesis 1:20–25

The fish were created out of the sea and for the sea; the cattle and other beasts of the earth were created out of the earth and for the earth. The whole of creation was based on the principle of environment, and the same principle applied to the creation of man. Man was created out of an environment and for an environment. "And God said, Let us make man in our image, after our likeness: and let them have dominion over the fish of the sea, and over the fowl of the air, and over the cattle, and over all the earth, and over every creeping thing that creepeth upon the earth. So God created man in his own image, in the image of God created he him; male and female created he them" (Genesis 1:26–27). "And the LORD God formed man of the dust of the ground, and breathed into his nostrils the breath of life; and man became a living soul" (Genesis 2:7). Man's body was made from the earth, but his spirit, the real man, came from God. Just as God spoke to the water and the earth to bring forth according to their kind, so also He spoke to Himself and brought us forth according to His own kind. God being three in one (Trinity) said, "Let us make man in our image and likeness"; the real man was created in God but put in a body that was made from the earth. Note that God did not speak to the earth to bring forth man because the real man had already been created in God. The body that came from the earth qualified man to live on earth, while the spirit that came from God qualified man to live in the presence of God (the Spirit of God). Therefore, man's environment before the fall was the presence of God on earth. This is what the garden of Eden represented. It was the spot on earth where the presence of God was. What made the garden of Eden important was simply the presence of God. The Tree of Life was in the garden because the presence of God was there. You can never find the Tree of Life outside the presence of God. "It is the spirit that quickeneth; the flesh profiteth nothing: the words that I speak unto you, they are spirit, and they are life" (John 6:63). The greatest thing man lost when he sinned was the presence of God, and it happened in two ways. Firstly, the presence of God upon man lifted, and man became flesh. Secondly, man was driven out of the presence of God as an environment, which the garden represented. When man sinned, he lost the presence of God on his life, and when he was driven out of the garden he lost the presence of God as an environment. In the new birth, God, in His mercy, has also taken care of the loss in two ways: the Spirit is in us, and we are in the Spirit. "And I will pray the Father, and he shall give you another Comforter, that he may abide with you forever; even the Spirit of truth; whom the world cannot receive, because it seeth him not, neither knoweth him:

37

but ye know him; **for he dwelleth with you, and shall be in you**" (John 14:16–17, emphasis added). "For by one Spirit are we all baptized into one body, whether we be Jews or Gentiles, whether we be bond or free; and have been all made to drink into one Spirit" (1 Corinthians 12:13). It is very important that we understand the fact that the Spirit of God is our new environment. There is life only within the Spirit; everything outside the Spirit is death. All that God has for us are available only in the Spirit. "Blessed be the God and Father of our Lord Jesus Christ, who hath blessed us with all spiritual blessings in heavenly places in Christ" (Ephesians 1:3). Remember that *Christ* means "the anointed one," one who is full of the Holy Spirit or one who is covered with the presence of God. We can say that all that God has done or provided for us are available only in Christ, the anointed one, and it is only as we become one with Him that they become ours. Generally, created beings function effectively only in the environment for which they were created, and they will naturally malfunction outside that environment. Just imagine a fish trying to live on the ground or a bird trying to live in water. So also the new man can function properly only in the Spirit or in Christ. "For the kingdom of God is not meat and drink; but righteousness, and peace, and joy in the Holy Ghost" (Romans 14:17). The Holy Spirit is the environment of the kingdom of God, and by the new birth we have been translated into the kingdom. "Giving thanks unto the Father, which hath made us meet to be partakers of the inheritance of the saints in light: who hath delivered us from the power of darkness, and hath translated us into the kingdom of his dear Son" (Colossians 1:12–13). In fact, we are children of the kingdom. The good news is that if you are born again, you are already in the Spirit, and all you need is to begin to walk in the Spirit. Just as all Adam and Eve needed to live in the garden was provided free, all we need to live now have been provided free in the Spirit (Ephesians 1:3). Walking in the Spirit is a must for us. It is the only environment where proper functioning and effectiveness are guaranteed for a Christian. It is also the only environment where we can actually be useful and pleasing to God in all that we do.

5. We Mature Through the Leading of the Holy Spirit

"For as many as are led by the Spirit of God, they are the sons of God" (Romans 8:14). If you are ever to become a son of God as distinct from a child of God, you must be led by the Spirit. Spiritual growth and maturity are possible only as the Holy Spirit leads us. There is no other way to mature spiritually. Anyone who truly seeks spiritual maturity must submit to the leading of the Holy Spirit, and the leading of the Spirit is possible only as we walk in the Spirit. "For what man knoweth the things of a man, save the spirit of man which is in him? Even so the things of God knoweth no man, but the Spirit of God" (1 Corinthians 2:11). No man knows the things of God except the Holy Spirit. He is the only one who can lead us safely to our destination in Christ. That is why we are admonished not to grieve Him. "And grieve not the holy Spirit of God, whereby ye are sealed unto the day of redemption" (Ephesians 4:30). We must never forget that it is only as we are led by the Spirit that we are not under the law. "But if ye be led of the Spirit, ye are not under the law" (Galatians 5:18).

6. Jesus has handed us over to the Holy Spirit.

"Nevertheless I tell you the truth; It is expedient for you that I go away: for if I go not away, the Comforter will not come unto you; but if I depart, I will send him unto you....Howbeit when he, the Spirit of truth, is come, he will guide you into all truth: for he shall not speak of himself; but whatsoever he shall hear, that shall he speak: and he will shew you things to come. He shall glorify me: for he shall receive of mine, and shall shew it unto you. All things that the Father hath are mine: therefore said I, that he shall take of mine, and shall shew it unto you."
—John 16:7,13–15

The Holy Spirit is the one currently here with us on earth. He is everything to us. He is our teacher, guide, helper, and even our environment. "Likewise the Spirit also helpeth our infirmities: for we know not what we should pray for as we ought: but the Spirit itself maketh intercession for us with groanings which cannot be uttered" (Romans 8:26). Thus, the Holy Spirit has a ministry to fulfill in our lives, and it is only as we walk in the Spirit that this ministry of the Holy Spirit is fulfilled in our lives.

> "But as it is written, Eye hath not seen, nor ear heard, neither have entered into the heart of man, the things which God hath prepared for them that love him. But God hath revealed them unto us by his Spirit: for the Spirit searcheth all things, yea, the deep things of God. For what man knoweth the things of a man, save the spirit of man which is in him? even so the things of God knoweth no man, but the Spirit of God. Now we have received, not the spirit of the world, but the spirit which is of God; that we might know the things that are freely given to us of God."
> —1 Corinthians 2:9–12

Without the Holy Spirit there will be no Christianity because we will be like orphans without the father. Walking in the Spirit enable us to function as redesigned or recreated.

7. The whole world lies under the control of the Devil.

"We know that we are children of God, and that the whole world is under the control of the evil one" (1 John 5:19 NIV). Many of us are yet to come to terms with the fact that the whole world is under the control of the Devil. If we really understand and accept this fact, our attitude toward this world will change. The reason why we are devoting so much time to the world and the things of the world is because we have yet to realize that the whole world is under the control of the Devil. In fact, Jesus called him "the ruler of this world" (John 14:30 RSV). Have you never marveled that though God created the world, He has warned us not to love the world or the things in it? "Love not the world, neither the things that are in the world. If any man loves the world, the love of the Father is not in him. For all that is in the world, the lust of the flesh, and the lust of the eyes, and the pride of life, is not of the Father, but is of the world. And the world passeth away, and the lust thereof: but he that doeth the will of God abideth forever" (1 John 2:15–17).

It is dangerous to love the world because it amounts to submitting to the Devil who has control or rules over the whole world. Please, don't confuse the control of the world with the ownership. The earth and its fullness still belong to the Lord, and as a result He can provide all we need and do whatever He wants to do. Making us love the world is the subtle way the Devil seek to lure us back under his control after we have been delivered from his kingdom (Colossians 1:13). As far as God is concerned, we are no longer of this world. "I have given them thy word; and the world hath hated them, because they are not of the world, even as I am not of the world. I pray not that thou shouldest take them out of the world, but that thou shouldest keep them from the evil. They are not of the world, even as I am not of the world" (John 17:14–16). We must understand and appreciate the fact that we are *not* of this world. We have been saved from this world; let us not put ourselves into bondage again to the world. God has not given us the world for an inheritance; rather, the world is being kept for destruction. "For this they willingly are ignorant of, that by the word of God the heavens were of old, and the earth standing out of the water and in the water: Whereby the world that then was, being overflowed with water, perished: But the heavens and the earth, which are now, by the same word are kept in store, reserved unto fire against the day of judgment and perdition of ungodly men" (2 Peter 3:5–7). In the days of Noah, the only things that survived the water were the ark and the earth; every other thing was destroyed. God has again declared that the present world will be destroyed, but this time even the earth will be burned. "But the day of the Lord will come as a thief in the night; in the which the heavens shall pass away with a great noise, and the elements shall melt with fervent heat, the earth also and the works that are therein shall be burned up" (2 Peter 3:10). It is only ignorance that can keep us bound to this world just like people in the days of Noah. The Devil uses the world to control mankind through the flesh. Put in another way, walking in the flesh keeps us under the control of the Devil through the power of the world. The good news is that if we are born of God, we have been empowered to overcome the world

"For whatsoever is born of God overcometh the world: and this is the victory that overcometh the world, even our faith" (1 John 5:4). Without the flesh it will be impossible for the devil and the world to have power over man. Walking in the Spirit protects us from the flesh and its influence. "This I say then, Walk in the Spirit, and ye shall not fulfil the lust of the flesh" (Galatians 5:16). It is as we walk in the Spirit that we can avoid fulfilling the desires of the flesh. Walking in the Spirit is the only way we can be in this world and not live according to this world. It is also the only way we cannot fall in love with the world and the things in the world.

8. The flesh profits nothing.

This is another serious reason why we must walk in the Spirit. Obviously, no normal human being wants to labor in vain. "It is the spirit that quickeneth; the flesh profiteth nothing: the words that I speak unto you, they are spirit, and they are life" (John 6:63). Jesus speaking here made it clear that the flesh profits nothing. The flesh does not benefit us in any way. The truth we must understand is that there is no free zone between the Spirit, and the flesh. It is either we are walking in the flesh or we are walking in the Spirit, and everything done in the flesh is useless. Whether the labor is to achieve obedience, holiness, or perform service, once it is of the flesh, it is a wasted effort because it reveals a dependence on self rather than God. "Then he answered and spake unto me, saying, This is the word of the LORD unto Zerubbabel, saying, Not by might, nor by power, but by my spirit, saith the LORD of hosts" (Zechariah 4:6). Walking in the flesh is the greatest manifestation and evidence of unbelief in the life of a Christian.

9. Make no provision for the flesh.

"But put ye on the Lord Jesus Christ, and make not provision for the flesh, to fulfil the lusts thereof" (Romans 13:14). Here we are admonished to put on Christ and not to make way for the flesh. We should not give the flesh any chance at all because it is dangerous; though it is dead and buried, it has the capacity to wake up once the atmosphere is created. Don't forget that your body is still the burial place of your dead flesh. You have a responsibility to keep it buried by not allowing things that could arouse it back to action in your life. Walking in the Spirit is the only way we can keep the flesh dead and buried.

CHAPTER 4

FURTHER
UNDERSTANDING OF
WALKING
IN THE SPIRIT

IN CHAPTERS 1 and 2, we said that true or complete obedience, which is required for a successful Christian life, is a product of the Spirit, which manifests as we walk in the Spirit. We also emphasized that God, knowing that none of us can ever achieve the obedience or righteousness required to enable His grace reign in our lives, made us obedient by the obedience of Jesus (Romans 5:19). It is just as we were made disobedient by the natural birth that we have also been made obedient by the new birth. The issue of obedience was emphasized because if not put in proper perspective, it becomes a serious hindrance to walking in the Spirit. The acceptable acts of obedience are those produced by faith. In Chapter 3, we looked at some of the reasons why we must walk in the Spirit. Some of the reasons we identified are, God is spirit and we can worship Him only in Spirit and in truth (John 4:23–24). We have become spirit beings because we have been born of the Spirit (John 3:5–6). We have also become one spirit with the Lord (1 Corinthians 6:17); and finally, we emphasized that the Spirit has become our new habitat, environment, or dwelling place (Romans 8:9). As a result, the Spirit is the only environment where we can function properly and effectively. In this chapter, we shall move deeper into the study by considering the following subtopics:

- What does it mean to walk in the Spirit?
- Walking in the Spirit and the flesh
- How can we walk in the Spirit?

WHAT DOES IT MEAN TO WALK IN THE SPIRIT?

To walk in the Spirit is to walk in the presence of God, that is, to walk immersed in God. Note that the Bible does not say we should walk *with* the Spirit but to walk *in* the Spirit. "For in him we live, and move, and have our being; as certain also of your own poets have said, For we are also his offspring" (Acts 17:28). Note the word *in* it is of great significance in this study. The word *walking* is not referring to what we do when we use our feet to advance in movement, but it implies activities in the Spirit that produce definite actions in the physical. "If we live in the Spirit, let us also walk in the Spirit" (Galatians 5:25). To walk in the Spirit is to carry out activities in the Spirit. As we have seen, at the new birth the Spirit becomes our new environment, that is, our dwelling place or home. To walk in the Spirit is to move according to the will, the direction, and the predetermined movement pattern of the Spirit, who has become our new home or environment. Thus, to walk in the Spirit is to flow with the Holy Spirit or, as we have described it earlier, to follow the leading of the Holy Spirit. You walk in the Spirit when you accept and comply with the leading of the Holy Spirit, which amounts to flowing in or with the Holy Spirit. Your flow in or with the Holy Spirit is a function of how much you are full of the Spirit.

> "Afterward he brought me again unto the door of the house; and, behold, waters issued out from under the threshold of the house eastward: for the forefront of the house stood toward the east, and the waters came down from under from the right side of the house, at the south side of the altar. Then brought he me out of the way of the gate northward, and led me about the way without unto the utter gate by the way that looketh eastward; and, behold, there ran out waters on the right side. And when the man that had the line in his hand went forth eastward, he measured

a thousand cubits, and he brought me through the waters; the waters were to the ankles. Again he measured a thousand, and brought me through the waters; the waters were to the knees. Again he measured a thousand, and brought me through; the waters were to the loins. Afterward he measured a thousand; and it was a river that I could not pass over: for the waters were risen, waters to swim in, a river that could not be passed over."
—Ezekiel 47:1–7

The water that issues from the altar is a type of the anointing. There is a "volume or measure" of anointing that you need to float in the Spirit. If you operate below that measure, you will struggle with the Spirit, and your advancement/operation will be hindered. Let us follow the various levels of anointing demonstrated in the above Scripture. The first level was ankle deep; at ankle deep though you are in the water; apart from wetting your feet, it does not have any influence over you. Ankle-deep anointing will also not have any influence over you though you are in the Spirit. The next level is loins or waist deep; at this level the water is beginning to affect your movement or have influence on you. Waist-deep anointing is the level where the Holy Spirit has minimal influence over you, and at this level you can still struggle in the Spirit. The third and final level is a river that cannot be crossed except by swimming; here the water is able to exert its full impact on you without really directly controlling you; you either recognize the nature of the water, or you will pay dearly for doing otherwise. The same applies to the anointing; it is only when we are full of the Spirit that the Spirit can exert His full impact upon us without necessarily controlling us. At this level all our decisions will be influenced by the Holy Spirit. Then we will be said to be led by the Spirit and therefore walking in the Spirit. Walking in the Spirit can also be likened to walking in any other environment such as walking on earth, swimming in water, floating in space, and so forth. The forces of the environment determine the movement pattern and set the parameters for the movement without hindering our power of choice. As a result you can advance only as you utilize or submit to these forces. The same principle applies in walking in the Spirit; that is why we can say that to walk in the Spirit is to move according to the predetermined pattern and within the parameters set for the movement by the Holy Spirit. In summary, walking in the Spirit is doing that which is of the Spirit, by the Spirit, and in the Spirit but without being forced or compelled to do so. By walking in the Spirit you willingly submit to the Holy Spirit, allowing Him to accomplish His work in you. That is why the Bible says, "For it is God which worketh in you both to will and to do of his good pleasure" (Philippians 2:13).

WALKING IN THE SPIRIT AND THE FLESH

The flesh is the major hindrance to walking in the Spirit, and until we deal with the flesh, we can never walk in the Spirit, and walking in the Spirit is the proof that we have crucified the flesh. "This I say then, Walk in the Spirit, and ye shall not fulfil the lust of the flesh. For the flesh lusteth against the Spirit, and the Spirit against the flesh: and these are contrary the one to the other: so that ye cannot do the things that ye would. But if ye be led of the Spirit, ye are not under the law" (Galatians 5:16–18). The flesh here is referring to the human nature without God. Before we accepted Christ as Lord and master, the flesh was in charge; it was the source of all our actions, behaviors, and attitudes. Put in another way, our actions were a fulfillment of the desires of the flesh. Though the flesh is no longer in charge, it is constantly looking out for an opportunity to take over again, even if temporarily; that is why the flesh is always at war against the Spirit according to the above Scripture. There are two distinct ways in which the flesh hinders our walk in the Spirit:

- The flesh as the flesh
- The actions of the body as a result of past submissions to the flesh.

When the flesh is alive (active), it is a hindrance to walking in the Spirit because it was the real you before you became born again. Generally speaking, you are the sum total of all that you believed. This is a truth we must never forget. You are what you believe

48

because what you believe operates you; that is, what you believe determine your actions, behavior, and attitude. What you believe determines your response to situations and circumstances. It can be likened to the computer program or software without which the computer, no matter how sophisticated, becomes a dummy. Just as what the computer can do is determined by the software loaded in it, so also what we can do is determined by what we have believed. Everything you believed outside God constitutes the flesh. We can say that the flesh is the sum total of everything we have believed that is not of God that produces ways of life and attitudes which eventually determine our response to situations and circumstances. *We must understand that the flesh is not another being that lives within us;* rather, it is our product achieved through the influence of the Devil working directly on us or through the world and its systems, such as cultures, traditions, and ways of life that are generally contrary to the Word of God. When a child is born depending on the environment created by the parents or the environment where they live and the spirits operating in the area, the flesh begins to be formed. The formation of the flesh continues throughout the life of a man unless he gets born again and turns from his old ways by submitting to the Holy Spirit. The flesh is the product of all the things you have come to believe, that is, the things you have accepted as true and real, out of all the things that were presented to you by spirits, people, culture, physical environment, and so on. Whatever you believed, that is, accepted as a true and real way of life, became your flesh. It ruled your life and determined your actions and attitudes. We should not confuse the flesh with demonic possession, which enables evil spirits to express themselves through man. Take the example of anger, which is a common problem with many people. Anger can be a work of the flesh and can also be an expression of the spirit of anger. As a work of the flesh, it is your manifestation, but as an expression of evil spirits, it is a direct manifestation of the spirit of anger, in which case you will usually not be in control. That is, you cannot control how and when it occurs, and most times you will regret after it is over. The flesh is our product, and that is what makes it so dangerous. We make the mistake of thinking and accepting it as our real nature even after the new birth. As long as it is alive, you cannot walk effectively in the spirit because its works are contrary to the manifestations of the Holy Spirit. "Now the works of the flesh are manifest, which are these; Adultery, fornication, uncleanness, lasciviousness, idolatry, witchcraft, hatred, variance, emulations, wrath, strife, seditions, heresies, envyings, murders, drunkenness, revellings, and such like: of the which I tell you before, as I have also told you in time past, that they which do such things shall not inherit the kingdom of God" (Galatians 5:19–21). That is not to say that all of the above must be present before it is flesh. What you have in your flesh will depend on the influence you received. God's solution to the issue of the flesh is death. "Mortify therefore your members which are upon the earth; fornication, uncleanness, inordinate affection, evil concupiscence, and covetousness, which is idolatry" (Colossians 3:5). Until the flesh is put to death, walking in the spirit will be a struggle.

Now the second way the flesh hinders our walk in the Spirit is by the actions of the body as a result of past submissions to the flesh. Before we came to Jesus, our physical bodies usually take instructions from the flesh, and after performing such instructions so often, the body adjusts and begins to perform them automatically any time the conditions or situation arises. It becomes an unconscious act where your body no longer has to wait for instructions from the flesh. This is how behaviors and addictions begin. **Your body will usually get used to whatever you make it perform regularly.** As a result, after the new birth, the body will naturally continue to perform all the actions the flesh has taught it anytime the conditions and situations arise. This is a serious hindrance to walking in the Spirit, and that is why we are admonished to present our bodies to God "I beseech you therefore, brethren, by the mercies of God, that ye present your bodies a living sacrifice, holy, acceptable unto God, which is your reasonable service" (Romans 12:1). It is only by a complete surrender of the body to the Holy Spirit that we can be delivered from this problem. Presenting the body is a service God requires of every believer. To present your body means to consciously release the activities of the body to the Holy Spirit, who dwells in you. "What? know ye not that your body is the temple of the Holy Ghost which is in you, which ye have of God, and ye are not your own? For ye are bought with a price: therefore glorify God in your body, and in your spirit, which are God's" (1 Corinthians 6:19–20). Put in another way, presenting your body means not to allow your body to perform activities that do not glorify God. Any activity of the body that you have not released to the Holy Spirit becomes an opening for the flesh and the Devil. To walk effectively in the Spirit, the flesh and all its remedial activities must be eliminated. The measure to which you succeed in eliminating them is the measure to which you can effectively walk in the Spirit. Unfortunately, the flesh cannot be eliminated completely until we are finally transformed into His likeness (1 John3:2). That is why Jesus admonished us to pick up our crosses daily as we follow Him. Meaning, you must reestablish the death of your flesh daily. "Then said Jesus unto his disciples, If any man will come after me, let him deny himself, and take up his cross, and follow me" (Matthew 16:24). To deal with your flesh, you must learn by the power of the Holy Spirit to say no to the desires of the flesh while exercising faith in your codeath with Christ at Calvary.

Our Codeath with Christ

"For you died, and your life has been hidden with Christ in God" (Colossian 3:3). Most Christians have come to understand and appreciate the spiritual death that occurred when Adam and Eve disobeyed God at the garden of Eden, but not many understand that there has also been a physical death for all of mankind. There can be no meaningful spiritual growth until we understand and properly appropriate the death of Jesus as it relates to our lives and the entire human existence. Many over the years have seen the death of Jesus only as a substitute to pay for our sin or to bring us salvation. This is correct, but it is just half of the truth because it does not bring out the entire reality and substance of what actually happened at Calvary. If you can understand or capture what actually happened at Calvary, it will change the way you see everything in this world.

First and foremost, we need to understand that Jesus did not only die in our place or for us as we have come to understand what happened at Calvary. That is, His death is not just a substitution for the death we should have died. What happened at Calvary has much more serious impact on our lives and the whole of creation than that understanding presents. To appreciate and see the reality of the impact on our lives, we must understand the depth of what happened. The death of Jesus is both good news and bad news depending on where you are looking at it from or which side of it you are on. It is good news if you accept God's salvation plan associated with it, but it is bad news if you choose to ignore the salvation so graciously offered by God. Now to the point, what God is saying to us is that we died with Christ at Calvary not in terms of substitution but in the real sense of the word. It is important and vital that you understand that you really died in Christ at Calvary because it will enable you to appreciate the reality of the old and the new in Christ. Now, let's try to explain it in a logical sequence: when Jesus died at Calvary, everything that was in Him died. To appreciate this fact, we must understand who He is and what was in Him. Now, remember that Jesus is the Word of God that became flesh. "In the beginning was the Word, and the Word was with God, and the Word was God" ....And the Word was made flesh, and dwelt among us, (and we beheld his glory, the glory as of the only begotten of the Father,) full of grace and truth" (John 1:1–14). Which means the person who died at Calvary was the Word of God that became flesh bearing the name Jesus. The Bible also says that "all things were made by him; and without him was not any thing made that was made" (John 1:3). That means the person who died at Calvary was the same person by whom God created all things including mankind. John 1:4 also says, "In him was life; and the life was the light of men," meaning that the same person who died was the one in whom the life of mankind resided. The Bible also says, "For by him were all things created, that are in heaven, and that are in earth, visible and invisible, whether they be thrones, or dominions, or principalities, or powers: all things were created by him, and for him" (Colossians 1:16). The central truth of this verse is that everything that is created was created by Jesus and they belong to Him. So the person who died is the same one who owns everything that was created. That is why the Bible says He came to His own, but His own did not receive Him. "He came unto his own, and his own received him not" (John 1:11). Now to the main point, the Bible. Colossians 1:17 says, "And he is before all things, and by him all things consist." The word *consist* means that things are held together or reside or continue in Him. Since everything that was created was spoken into existence, they are products of the Word of God. We can say that the Word of God (Jesus) is the spiritual material everything is made of, and they are also sustained, kept, and continue in Him. The central thought here is that everything that was created was created by the Word of God, for the Word of God, and they exist and continue to by the same Word of God. This is the same as saying that everything that was created was created by Jesus, and for Jesus and they exist by Him, and their continuity is guaranteed only in Him.

We can therefore say that when God decided to send Jesus (His Word) into the world to die, He was putting an end to everything that was associated with the creation that began with the earth as recorded in the book of Genesis. Thus at the death of Jesus, mankind and everything associated with it died. The existence of the present world as created by God officially ended when Jesus died. The time between the death of Jesus and the eventual end of the world, as already documented in the book of Revelation, is what the scientist calls the "stopping distance". For those who may not understand the term "stopping distance", it refers to the time it takes to stop a body in motion after the brakes have been applied. This principle is actually visible in all of creation. For example, if you cut a branch from a tree, the branch does not die instantly; rather, death will begin to show on the branch after about three days depending on the kind of tree. We also see this principle at play when Adam and Eve sinned and lost the everlasting life; the life span of mankind gradually diminished from almost a thousand years to what we have today. It was the same stopping distance principle that was at work then. The world as we know and now see it ended spiritually two thousand years ago when Jesus died at Calvary. That is why the book of Revelation has clearly outlined the events that will finally bring the world to an end. Things happen in the spirit before they manifest physically. Your codeath with Jesus is a reality whether you understand it or not, but you need to understand it to enjoy the benefit. The reality of our codeath with Christ at Calvary must remain in our consciousness to be established in our lives. Second Corinthians 5:14 says, "For the love of Christ constraineth us; because we thus judge, that if one died for all, then were all dead." This Scripture emphasizes that if one died for all, then all died because, as we have seen already, the one who died is the same one by whom all things exist. The question you must answer for yourself is, when the one by whom all things exists died, what happened to the thing that exists by Him? The simple answer will be, it died. We cannot overemphasize the fact that everything died in Christ because it is the simple and basic truth that must be understood to put all things in their proper perspective. When Jesus died at Calvary, everything died including you and me. Our ability to walk in the Spirit and effectiveness in the Christian walk are heavily dependent on the fact of our codeath with Christ. The major reason many of us are still struggling with our Christian lives is because we have not been established in the fact of our codeath with Christ. The true and proper beginning of the Christian walk is the passing away of the old. "Therefore if any man be in Christ, he is a new creature: old things are passed away; behold, all things are become new" (2 Corinthians 5:17). The old really passes away only as we are established in the fact of our codeath with Christ. Let me ask you, have you seen a dead man who gets angry, greedy, or drunk or who fornicates or commits any other sin? If you find one, let me know. *The only key to manifesting the new life is the appropriation of our codeath with Jesus by faith.* The new cannot manifest beyond the level you have allowed the old to pass away. That is why we are admonished to reckon ourselves dead unto sin. "Likewise reckon ye also yourselves to be dead indeed unto sin, but alive unto God through Jesus Christ our Lord" (Romans 6:11). To reckon yourself dead means to count or consider yourself to be dead indeed or to accept as true the fact that you have died in Christ. It is not asking you to assume that you died but that you keep yourself in the reality of your actual death in Christ. That is why Jesus also admonished us to take up our cross daily as we follow Him. "And he said to them all, If any man will come after me, let him deny himself, and take up his cross daily, and follow me" (Luke 9:23). You cannot really follow Jesus in the new life without establishing the fact of your codeath with Him. Note that it is the fact of our codeath with Jesus that water baptism is expected to establish. "Know ye not, that so many of us as were baptized into Jesus Christ were baptized into his death. Therefore we are buried with him by baptism into death: that like as Christ was raised up from the dead by the glory of the Father, even so we also should walk in newness of life" (Romans 6:3–4). You can never walk in the Spirit or live effectively as a Christian beyond the level you have appropriated and allowed your codeath with Jesus to manifest in your life.

OUR LIFE IS HIDDEN IN CHRIST

After we have understood the fact of our codeath with Christ, we must also understand that we now have a new life and that this new life is not in us but hidden in Him. "For you died, and your life has been hidden with Christ in God" (Colossians 3:3 NJKV). The greatest hindrance to effective Christian living is the fear of losing our lives. We put a lot of effort into trying to protect our lives because of lack of knowledge. The truth is, when you accepted Jesus as your Lord and personal Savior, you gave Him your life in order to receive the new life He has offered. Now that new life is in Him; that is, Christ Himself is your new life, and without Him you have no life. Thus, if you are a child of God, your life is not with you, but it is hidden in Christ for you. It is only when He appears that your life will appear. "Your real life is Christ and when he appears, then you too will appear with him and share his glory" (Colossians 3:4 GNT). Without Christ you have no life because all of mankind died in Him at Calvary. That is what Jesus meant when He declared, "I am the way, the truth, and the life; no one goes to the Father except by me" (John 14:6 NIV). You do not have to worry about your life right now because the life you live now is not directly in you but in Christ, who is in you, and it is to be lived only by faith in Him. This is what apostle Paul meant when he said, "I am crucified with Christ: nevertheless I live; yet not I, but Christ liveth in me: and the life which I now live in the flesh I live by the faith of the Son of God, who loved me, and gave himself for me" (Galatians 2:20). That is also the reason why the Bible says the just shall live by faith (Romans 1:17). You cannot really live by faith until you understand that the life you are to live now is Christ. The foundation of faith is the understanding that the life we have now is Christ Himself, "Your real life is Christ" (Colossians 3:4 GNT). That is why the Bible places a lot of emphasis on our abiding in Him because we have become a part of Him and are one Spirit with Him. The reality of our codeath with Christ and the understanding that our lives are hidden in Him are the only ways the fear of death will not continue to hold us captive. "And deliver them who through fear of death were all their lifetime subject to bondage" (Hebrews 2:15). Walking in the Spirit will not be possible without a proper understanding of our codeath with Christ and the fact that our new life is hidden in Him.

HOW TO WALK IN THE SPIRIT

As already declared, to walk in the Spirit is to do that which is of the Spirit, by the Spirit, and in the Spirit. The question is, how do we who live in the physical really begin to do that which is of the Spirit, by the Spirit, and in the Spirit? The answer is a single word: faith. Thus, to walk in the Spirit is to walk by faith. Remember that we are the sum total of all that we believe, and to walk by faith is to walk in line with the Word of God that we have believed. To walk by faith, therefore, is to live and act according to the truths received by revelation from the Holy Spirit. The beauty of it is that such truths received from the Holy Spirit are able to produce the required action in us because every revealed truth or word has the capacity to execute or perform itself. Such revealed truths also operate very much like the computer program which once installed will continue to execute itself. Faith releases the power to perform because it is the spiritual program (sets of believes) that the Holy Spirit is able to load into us. "This is the covenant that I will make with them after those days, saith the Lord, I will put my laws into their hearts, and in their minds will I write them" (Hebrews 10:16). Now, understand that this Scripture is not referring to the Laws of Moses because God was talking about a new covenant. The law that He wants to write in our hearts can be more appropriately described as the spiritual programs (sets of believes) by which we will function like Him, and this is what faith is all about. What the Holy Spirit can do with us is limited to this spiritual program called faith that we have allowed Him to load into us. It is when we function by this spiritual programs called faith that our actions can be said to be of the Spirit, by the Spirit, and in the Spirit. The Bible actually refers to this spiritual program as the law of the spirit of life in Christ Jesus. "There is therefore now no condemnation to them which are in Christ Jesus, who walk not after the flesh, but after the Spirit. For **the law of the Spirit of life in Christ Jesus** hath made me free from the law of sin and death" (Romans 8:1–2, emphasis added). Note that this law is available only to those who walk in the Spirit because if you continue to walk in the flesh you will remain under condemnation. Thus, to walk in the Spirit is to submit to the law of the Spirit of life in Christ Jesus, which is also known as the law of faith. "Where is boasting then? It is excluded. By what law? of works? Nay: but by the law of faith. Therefore we conclude that a man is justified by faith without the deeds of the law" (Romans 3:27–28). The law of the Spirit of life in Christ Jesus is the law of faith, and until it is written in your heart and mind, you really do not have faith, and you cannot walk in the Spirit. If you do not have faith, you are not justified, meaning you are still under condemnation. Can you begin to appreciate why faith is, no doubt, the most critical element of the Christian walk? That is why it is impossible to please God without faith. "But without faith it is impossible to please him: for he that cometh to God must believe that he is, and that he is a rewarder of them that diligently seek him." (Hebrews 11:6). You can never please God until you allow Him to write the law of the Spirit of life in Christ Jesus into your heart and mind. That is, your ability to please God depends on your allowing Him to write the law of the Spirit of life in Christ Jesus in your heart and mind. This will help you to understand what the Bible means by "the just shall live by faith." "Now the just shall live by faith: but if any man draw back, my soul shall have no pleasure in him" (Hebrews 10:38). "For therein is the righteousness of God revealed from faith to faith: as it is written, the just shall live by faith" (Romans 1:17). To be just you must live by faith, which means you must function by the law of the Spirit of life in Christ Jesus, which the Holy Spirit loads into your life as you hear by the Word of God. That is why we must give faith more serious attention in order to make meaningful progress in the Christian walk. All that God has done for us can be activated/actualized only by faith, and the purpose of all the gift of service given to men is to bring us to unity of faith, "And he gave some, apostles; and some, prophets; and some, evangelists; and some, pastors and teachers; for the perfecting of the saints, for the work of the ministry, for the edifying of the body of Christ: Till we all come in the unity of the faith, and of the knowledge of the Son of God, unto a perfect man, unto the measure of the stature of the fulness of Christ" (Ephesians 4:11–13). Unfortunately, faith has been so much abused and misunderstood, which is why somebody can wake up in the morning and declare that he or she has faith without doing anything. A lot of well-meaning Christians just assume they have faith because they are expectant or anticipating that God will do something for them. Faith is a gift, but you must receive it. That is why the Bible says, "Faith comes by hearing and hearing by the word of God" (Romans 10:17 NIV). Note that it says faith comes, which means faith was not there before then. If you have not heard, how can you say you have faith? Some also conclude that because they read the Bible they have faith. It is not just the hearing and hearing that matters but what happens during the hearing. No matter how long you have been

hearing, if that which hearing is supposed to produce is not produced, there will still be no faith. There is a process the Word must
undergo to release the Spirit of life in Christ Jesus; that is what
hearing and hearing is all about. Primarily, hearing and hearing
enable you to receive the content of the Word. "It is the spirit that
quickeneth; the flesh profiteth nothing: the words that I speak unto
you, they are spirit, and they are life" (John 6:63). Receiving the
Spirit and the life of the Word of God is the beginning of faith. After
we have received the Spirit and the life, the life must also release its
content, which includes light. "In the beginning was the Word, and
the Word was with God, and the Word was God. The same was in
the beginning with God. All things were made by him; and without
him was not any thing made that was made. In him was life; and
the life was the light of men" (John 1:1–4). We also receive the light
as we continue to hear and hear. "The entrance of thy words giveth
light; it giveth understanding unto the simple" (Psalm 119:130).
The purpose of the light is to lighten us. "That was the true Light,
which lighteth every man that cometh into the world" (John 1:9).
It is the light that brings understanding, enabling us to see the truth
and reality of what the Word is conveying to us. This will enable us
to receive the intangible form of what the Word is conveying, and
we will see it done though it has not yet manifested in the physical.
"Now faith is the substance of things hoped for, the evidence of
things not seen" (Hebrews 11:1). When the light of the Word is
released, the whole of our being is illuminated, the truth dawn on
us, and our hearts and minds are changed in line with the Word.
Faith comes from believing, and to believe is to accept something
as true and real. You can never accept the Word of God as true and
real until the light of the Word is released within you. The first evidence of faith is our confession. Once the light is released, you will
speak in line with that particular Word you received. However, the
process continues until the Word becomes the law of the Spirit of
life in Christ Jesus in our hearts. That is what enables us to always
speak and act according to our faith. In summary to have faith you
must learn to sow and be committed to sowing the seed of the Word
of God in your heart through consistent personal study/meditating

on the Word and fellowship with God, which enables you to receive the content of the Word as the seed is watered through prayer. There are several types and ways of praying, but we must emphasize that there is no other form of prayer that waters the seed of the Word to produce faith like praying in tongues. Faith is the exclusive work of the Holy Spirit in our lives. If you truly want to grow in faith, you must be committed to praying in tongues.

Praying in Tongues

Praying in tongues is a gift that God has provided to enable the Holy Spirit to intercede primarily for us through us. The Holy Spirit can and does intercede for us through other people when we are in trouble or facing one difficulty or the other, but the intercession for the release of faith for spiritual growth and advancement is usually through us. "Likewise the Spirit also helpeth our infirmities: for we know not what we should pray for as we ought: but the Spirit itself maketh intercession for us with groanings which cannot be uttered" (Romans 8:26). Note that the Holy Spirit intercedes for us not by talking to God on our behalf but by helping us speak to God miseries that we do not understand "For he that speaketh in an unknown tongue speaketh not unto men, but unto God: for no man understandeth him; howbeit in the spirit he speaketh mysteries" (1 Corinthians 14:2). God ordained this form of prayer to help bypass our understanding so that our limited understanding does not hinder what He can do with our lives or what the Word is conveying to us. Remember that the Word of God has inherent power to execute itself or to perform that for which God sent Him. "For as the rain cometh down, and the snow from heaven, and returneth not thither, but watereth the earth, and maketh it bring forth and bud, that it may give seed to the sower, and bread to the eater: So shall my word be that goeth forth out of my mouth: it shall not return unto me void, but it shall accomplish that which I please, and it shall prosper in the thing whereto I sent it" (Isaiah 55:10–11). Praying in tongues enables us to pray on the Word we have received such that the Word is watered to release its content unto us. If you have not received this gift of praying in tongues, you are cheating yourself. Note that we are not talking about the gift of prophesying in tongues. Praying in tongues and prophesying in tongues are two different things entirely. While the gift of speaking in tongues for prophecy is not for everybody, the gift of speaking in tongues in prayer is for everyone "Then Peter said unto them, Repent, and be baptized every one of you in the name of Jesus Christ for the remission of sins, and ye shall receive the gift of the Holy Ghost. For the promise is unto you, and to your children, and to all that are afar off, even as many as the Lord our God shall call" (Acts 2:38–39). Without this gift a Christian cannot make much progress though it is not every one who has received this gift that is making progress because how you use the gift is also very important. Some have received, but they are not using it, and so they are not making progress. You need to desire to receive and use this gift effectively if you are to make God's kind of progress. The truth is, when you pray in tongues, you are really edifying yourself. "He that speaketh in an unknown tongue edifieth himself; but he that prophesieth edifieth the church" (1 Corinthians 14:4). The word *edify,* according to the Webster's Dictionary, means to instruct and improve the mind in knowledge generally and particularly in moral and religious knowledge, in faith and holiness. Which means when you pray in tongues, you are actually instructing and improving your mind in the knowledge of God to release faith in the Word you have been studying. That is why the Bible says, "But ye, beloved, building up yourselves on your most holy faith, praying in the Holy Ghost" (Jude 1:20). If you want to do exploits by faith, you must learn to build up your faith through praying in tongues. Don't ever forget that praying in tongues is the major way the Holy Spirit helps us in our Christian walk. If you ignore or refuse to receive the gift of praying in tongues, you will be limiting the help you can receive from the Holy Spirit.

Let me give you another strong reason why praying in tongues is very important in the life of a Christian. Praying in tongues is the surest way the Holy Spirit can be in control of our tongues and begin the process of taming them. To present your body a living sacrifice unto God must start from the tongue.

"For in many things we offend all. If any man offend not in word, the same is a perfect man, and able also to bridle the whole body. Behold, we put bits in the horses' mouths, that they may obey us; and we turn about their whole body. Behold also the ships, which though they be so great, and are driven of fierce winds, yet are they turned about with a very small helm, whithersoever the governor listeth. Even so the tongue is a little member, and boasteth great things. Behold, how great a matter a little fire kindleth! And the tongue is a fire, a world of iniquity: so is the tongue among our members, that it defileth the whole body, and setteth on fire the course of nature; and it is set on fire of hell. For every kind of beasts, and of birds, and of serpents, and of things in the sea, is tamed, and hath been tamed of mankind: But the tongue can no man tame; it is an unruly evil, full of deadly poison."

—James 3:2–8

It is only with the help of the Holy Spirit that we can tame the tongue. "But if the Spirit of him that raised up Jesus from the dead dwell in you, he that raised up Christ from the dead shall also quicken your mortal bodies by his Spirit that dwelleth in you" (Romans 8:11). The more often we yield our tongues to the Holy Spirit in praying in tongues, the more He is able to tame it for us. If the Holy Spirit can control your tongue, your whole body will submit to Him. If you have not received this gift or if you have received it and are not using it effectively, you are hindering the work of the Spirit in your life, and walking in the Spirit will be a struggle. To receive is not difficult. All you have to do is desire it and ask God for it or ask somebody who has received it to lay hands on you. Note that desire comes through diligent study of the Bible and books that have been written on the issue. Praying in tongues is the easiest way to water the Word to enable its content to be released for our benefit. Our ability to believe is greatly enhanced when we know how to consciously and diligently water the Word by praying in tongues because praying in tongues enables the Holy Spirit to use the Word to change our wills and enables us to do according to the will of God.

CHAPTER 5

EVIDENCE OF
WALKING IN
THE SPIRIT

TO REFRESH OUR memories, let's quickly summarize the study so far. We have seen that true or complete obedience, which is required for a successful Christian life, is a product of the Spirit, which manifests as we walk in the Spirit. We emphasized that God, knowing that none of us can ever achieve the obedience or righteousness required to enable His grace reign in our lives, made us obedient by the obedience of Jesus or credited to us, at the new birth, the obedience of Jesus (Romans 5:19) . **We also saw that just as we were made disobedient by the natural birth, we have also been made obedient by the new birth.** The issue of obedience was emphasized because, if not put in proper perspective, it becomes a serious hindrance to walking in the Spirit. The only acceptable acts of obedience are those produced by faith. In Chapter 3, we looked at some of the reasons why we must walk in the Spirit. Some of the reasons we identified are these: God is spirit, and we can worship Him only in Spirit and in truth (John 4:23–24). We have become spirit beings because we have been born of the Spirit (John 3:5–6). We have also become one Spirit with the Lord (1 Corinthians 6:17), and finally, we emphasized that the Spirit has become our new habitat, environment, or dwelling place (Romans 8:9); and as a result, the Spirit is the only environment where we can function properly and effectively. In Chapter 4, we looked at the meaning of walking in the Spirit and emphasized that to walk in the Spirit is to walk in the presence of God, that is, to walk immersed in God. "For in him we live, and move, and have our being" (Acts 17:28a). Thus, to walk in the Spirit is to flow in the Spirit, that is, to be full of the Spirit till we willingly submit to the leading of the Holy Spirit (Romans 8:14). We also saw that to walk in the Spirit is to move according to the predetermined movement pattern and within the parameters set for the movement by the Holy Spirit. In summary, we said, walking in the Spirit is doing that which is of the Spirit, by the Spirit, and in the Spirit. We also said that walking in the Spirit is another way of saying submit to the Spirit and allow Him to accomplish His work in you. "For it is God which worketh in you both to will and to do of his good pleasure" (Philippians 2:13).

We also considered hindrances to walking in the Spirit and concluded that the flesh is the major hindrance. "This I say then, Walk in the Spirit, and ye shall not fulfil the lust of the flesh. For the flesh lusteth against the Spirit, and the Spirit against the flesh: and these are contrary the one to the other: so that ye cannot do the things that ye would. But if ye be led of the Spirit, ye are not under the law" (Galatians 5:16–18). We saw that we are the sum total of all that we believe, and everything we believed outside God constitutes the flesh. We said that the flesh is the sum total of all we have believed that resulted in our particular way of life and attitude, which eventually determined our response to situations and circumstances of life. We also said the flesh is our product achieved through the influence of the Devil working directly on us or through the world and its systems such as cultures and traditions.

We also considered how to walk in the Spirit, and we emphasized the importance of true faith, fullness of the Spirit, and praying in tongues in walking in the Spirit. We saw that praying in tongues is the easiest way to water the seed of the Word of God that enables it to release its content that results in faith, enabling us to function in line with the Word heard.

In this chapter, we shall proceed to examine the evidence of walking in the Spirit.

EVIDENCE OF WALKING IN THE SPIRIT

As we said earlier, walking in the Spirit is what we do as a result of being led by the Holy Spirit. That is why we said walking in the Spirit and being led by the Spirit are two sides of the same coin. The leading of the Holy Spirit does not manifest automatically in our lives; it manifests only when we accept and comply with it, and that is when we can be said to be walking in the Spirit. When you are led by the Spirit and you complete the process by walking in the Spirit, the eventual outcome is what we refer to as the evidence of walking in the Spirit. The evidence of walking in the Spirit has been summarized for us in 2 Timothy 1:7, which says, "For God hath not given us the spirit of fear; but of power, and of love, and of a sound mind". Thus, power, love, and sound mind are the evidences of walking in the Spirit. We can say that they are the proof that we are walking in the Spirit or that they are the result of the Holy Spirit's activities (Philippians 2:13 NIV) in our lives as we submit to Him. In fact, they are the very reason God put His Spirit in us and ordained that we should walk in Him. Power, love, and sound mind are His desired end products. The more of power, love, and sound mind we manifest, the more we are maturing and progressing toward becoming like Jesus. Beyond being our example, Jesus is our model or target; we are to conform to His likeness. "And we know that all things work together for good to them that love God, to them who are the called according to his purpose. For whom he did foreknow, he also did predestinate to be conformed to the image of his Son, that he might be the firstborn among many brethren" (Romans 8:28–29). Just as Jesus walked in the Spirit and the evidence was power, love, and sound mind, so also power, love, and sound mind will show in our lives as we progressively become like Him through walking in the Spirit. The greatest problem today is that Christians are unconsciously separating and choosing from these three evidences. Some give priority to love and disregard power, while others give priority to power at the expense of love, and yet others choose only sound mind (wisdom). This is what happens when we are not diligently and consistently walking in the Spirit. The true evidence of walking in the Spirit is a balance of the manifestation of the power, love, and mind of God in our lives.

POWER AS EVIDENCE

Power is the first evidence that we are walking in the Spirit. I am sure some of you will think I have made a mistake by putting power ahead of love. I assure you, there is no mistake at all; power comes before love though love is the ultimate. You cannot love until you have received the power. When you believe in Jesus, He does not give you love first but power. He gives you power to become or to manifest love. So believe me, power comes first, but love is the ultimate. Love without power is love in the flesh, which is totally unacceptable to God. The first thing that shows up in your life when you walk in the Spirit is power, and it is the power that enables you to release the other two evidences.

Therefore, the manifestation of the power of God in our lives is the first evidence that we are walking in the Spirit. "But you will receive power when the Holy Spirit comes on you; and you will be my witnesses in Jerusalem, and in all Judea and Samaria, and to the ends of the earth" (Acts 1:8). We have said that walking in the Spirit is possible only as we are full of the Spirit. The above Scripture is saying that we receive power when the Spirit comes upon us, and if I am walking in the Spirit, this power should show in my life. This power manifests in two distinct ways: in our lives to produce God's effects and through us to affect others. Many people misunderstand Acts 1:8; they conclude that the power received is for service only, contrary to what the Scripture is actually saying. According to the Scripture, the power shall make us witnesses. You cannot be an effective witness if the effect of the power is not evident in your own life. To confirm that you are walking in the Spirit, there must be evidence that the power of God is working in your life to affect and bless you, and through you to affect and bless others.

THE POWER OF GOD IN OUR LIVES

"But as many as received him, to them gave he power to become the sons of God, even to them that believe on his name" (John 1:12). Christianity is all about power and empowerment. In my first book titled *The Ultimate Purpose of Christianity*, it was emphasized that the ultimate purpose of Christianity is to produce the likeness of God in man. It was also emphasized that nothing exists without a purpose. Now, we can take a step further to say that things exist or are created to provide specific solutions or to meet specific needs. For a thing to achieve its purpose, it must be able to counter the need; that is, it must be empowered to overcome the need and produce the desired result. For example, the need for easy transportation led to the progressive invention of means of movement ranging from bicycle all the way to aircrafts. You will agree with me that in each case the purpose determined the power. There is an inherent power in every created thing to enable it to achieve its purpose. In the same way, there is an inherent power in Christianity to enable its purpose to be achieved. So also there is an inherent power God deposits in every Christian to enable him or her to fulfill the purpose of Christianity. Without this power, that person's Christianity is reduced to mere religion, and he or she will be struggling to satisfy God with the power of the flesh. That is why it is dangerous to believe in Christianity without believing in the power: "having a form of godliness but denying its power. And from such people turn away!" (2 Timothy 3:5 NIV). For the purpose of Christianity to be achieved in your life, you must receive and utilize the power of Christianity in your life. This power, according to John 1:12, is given only to those who have received Jesus and believe in His name. Let us understand that this power is in the Spirit of God. In fact, the Spirit of God is the power of God because if you ask God for power, He will simply give you the Holy Spirit: "Then he answered and spake unto me, saying, This is the word of the LORD unto Zerubbabel, saying, Not by might, nor by power, but by my spirit, saith the LORD of hosts" (Zechariah 4:6). If there is need for God to send power to you, He will simply send the Spirit, and you will receive power the moment the Spirit comes upon you

(Acts 1:8). Wherever the Spirit is, the power of God is also present. We can therefore safely say that the power of God is in the person of the Holy Spirit, and as a result we can apply and utilize the power of God only as we walk in the Spirit. We have said that the purpose of a thing determines the type and measure of power in it. For Christianity to be effective, it must have the type and measure of power necessary to achieve its purpose. Only the power of the Holy Spirit is sufficient to achieve the purpose of Christianity. To be effective as a Christian, you must have enough power to overcome the works of the Devil in and around your life. That is, you must have enough power to overcome sin, sickness, and poverty. These three manifestations of the Devil should progressively disappear from our lives if we are truly walking in the Spirit, in and by whom the power of God has been made available to us.

SIN

"Let not sin therefore reign in your mortal body, that ye should obey it in the lusts thereof. Neither yield ye your members as instruments of unrighteousness unto sin: but yield yourselves unto God, as those that are alive from the dead, and your members as instruments of righteousness unto God. For sin shall not have dominion over you: for ye are not under the law, but under grace" (Romans 6:12–14). Sin no longer has any authority to rule over us because its power over us was broken at Calvary. Instead we have been given power over sin, but that power is in the Holy Spirit and will manifest only as we walk in the Spirit.

> "There is therefore now no condemnation to them which are in Christ Jesus, who walk not after the flesh, but after the Spirit. For the law of the Spirit of life in Christ Jesus hath made me free from the law of sin and death. For what the law could not do, in that it was weak through the flesh, God sending his own Son in the likeness of sinful flesh, and for sin, condemned sin in the flesh: That the righteousness of the law might be fulfilled in us, who walk not after the flesh, but after the Spirit."
> —Romans 8:1–4

If you are walking in the Spirit, sin will have a hard job manifesting in your life. Concentrating on the Spirit and following His leading are a far more effective way of overcoming sin than struggling in your own effort. No matter how spiritual we become, sin will always try to show up in our lives, but our success in handling it will reveal how much we are walking in the Spirit and the level of power we are utilizing in the process. The level of power is a measure and a direct result of the level of our walk in the Spirit. So also the level of our victory over sin is a direct result of the level of our walk in the Spirit. Don't forget that Jesus has already paid the price for our sins. "And he is the propitiation for our sins: and not for ours only, but also for the sins of the whole world" (1 John 2:2). Jesus actually paid for the sins of the whole world, but it is only those who believe who will experience real freedom from sin. The level of your faith/walk in the Spirit determines the level of your freedom from sin. Don't be deceived; the wages of sin is always death whether for believer or unbeliever (Romans 6:23). If a believer continues in sin, he or she will surely pay because it is only those who through the Spirit mortify the deeds of the flesh who will enjoy eternal life at the end. "For if ye live after the flesh, ye shall die: but if ye through the Spirit do mortify the deeds of the body, ye shall live" (Romans 8:13). The truth is, if a child of God continues to live according to the flesh, which is the same as continuing in sin, even if ignorantly, he or she is still in danger of death. Which means he or she may not inherit the kingdom. Let's see another confirmation from Scripture. First Corinthians 6:19–20 states, "What? know ye not that your body is the temple of the Holy Ghost which is in you, which ye have of God, and ye are not your own? For ye are bought with a price: therefore glorify God in your body, and in your spirit, which are God's." As a result of the death of Jesus on the cross, we too have died to sin, and as result of His resurrection, we are empowered and expected to live unto righteousness (1 Peter 2:24).

SICKNESSES

"Who his own self bare our sins in his own body on the tree, that we, being dead to sins, should live unto righteousness: by whose stripes ye were healed" (1 Peter 2:24). As far as God is concerned, just as Jesus paid for the sin of the whole world, the sickness of the whole world has also been destroyed by His stripes (result of the beating before the crucifixion), but it is only those who believe and are walking in the Spirit who will experience true freedom from sickness. Jesus came to destroy the works of the Devil, and at the end He declared that it was finished. The power over sickness is available to everyone who believes, and it manifests as we walk in the Spirit. What many people fail to realize on the issue of sickness is that we were healed two thousand years ago when Jesus declared that it is finished, but the healing is activated as we walk in the Spirit. To put it in a simple way, it means that God, who knows the end from the beginning, packaged all the sicknesses and diseases that will ever come your way and put them on Jesus and then caused them to be knocked off His body by the unjust stripes He received in your place. That is to say, the power of sickness over your life has been broken such that, if you are walking in the correct level of power, when the sickness comes into your body, it will have no effect on you. "And these signs shall follow them that believe; In my name shall they cast out devils; they shall speak with new tongues; they shall take up serpents; and if they drink any deadly thing, it shall not hurt them; they shall lay hands on the sick, and they shall recover" (Mark 16:17). Instead of sickness having power over you, you will be dealing with sickness in others. What I am saying is, if you walk in the right level of power, any kind of disease can hit your body, but it will not be able to have effect upon you; your food may be poisoned, but it cannot kill you; or we may be in the midst of an epidemic, but you will not get hurt, and the word *sickness* will become foreign to you. This is God's desire for every one of us, but it is possible only as we walk in the Spirit because the Spirit is our true habitat, where we can function as recreated or to full capacity. I know that there are many people, like me, who are already increasingly enjoying this power over sicknesses. I encourage you to press toward total freedom from sicknesses, which is possible through a deeper and consistent walk in the Spirit.

POVERTY

"For ye know the grace of our Lord Jesus Christ, that, though he was rich, yet for your sakes he became poor, that ye through his poverty might be rich" (2 Corinthians 8:9). Jesus has also paid the price for our poverty such that we have no reason to remain poor. It is not God's desire that we continue in poverty. If we are increasingly becoming like Jesus, then we must come out of poverty. True deliverance from poverty comes as we walk in the Spirit. "But as it is written, Eye hath not seen, nor ear heard, neither have entered into the heart of man, the things which God hath prepared for them that love him" (1 Corinthians 2:9). It is as we walk in the Spirit that the Holy Spirit will show us what God has prepared for us. God wants us to have enough for ourselves, help others (until they enter into their own deliverance from poverty), and provide for the propagation of the gospel. Poverty should have no more power over you if you are truly walking in the Spirit. Giving, which is the foundation for prosperity, will become a part of you if you are indeed walking in the Spirit. In fact, you cannot walk in the Spirit and not be a giver.

Finally, if we are really walking in the Spirit, we will progressively manifest power over sin, sickness, poverty, and all other manifestations of the Devil; and their effects should progressively disappear from our lives. "Behold, I give unto you power to tread on serpents and scorpions, and over all the power of the enemy: and nothing shall by any means hurt you" (Luke 10:19). The power of God working in our lives is very important for witnessing. You cannot be an effective witness to what you have not experienced. The problem is that most of us are still operating in the realm of promise. We assume that God has just promised us deliverance, and so we are waiting for Him to fulfill His promise. Let me shock you by saying that if you are in Christ, God has not promised you deliverance. It is true that God promised Israel deliverance, but for you as a Christian He declares that you have been delivered. "Who hath delivered us from the power of darkness, and hath translated us into the kingdom of his dear Son" (Colossians 1:13). That is why you can become a new creature with old things passing away. "Therefore if any man be in Christ, he is a new creature: old things are passed away; behold, all things are become new" (2 Corinthians 5:17). As a new creature, sin, sicknesses, and poverty have no place in you except if you carelessly or ignorantly allow them.

THE POWER OF GOD WORKING THROUGH US

In addition to the power of God in our lives, the power must also work through us to impact the lives of others if we are truly walking in the Spirit. The will of God is to impact our lives with His power and also impact others through us. The Spirit is one place where the will of God always manifests. God has provided several definite gifts of the Spirit to enable His power to work through us to accomplish His will in the lives of the people around us and all the people He will bring in contact with us both Christians and non-Christians. "But the manifestation of the Spirit is given to every man to profit withal. For to one is given by the Spirit the word of wisdom; to another the word of knowledge by the same Spirit; to another faith by the same Spirit; to another the gifts of healing by the same Spirit; to another the working of miracles; to another prophecy; to another discerning of spirits; to another divers kinds of tongues; to another the interpretation of tongues: But all these worketh that one and the selfsame Spirit, dividing to every man severally as he will" (1 Corinthians 12:7–11). We cannot handle the gifts in detail now but we should note that the manifestations of the Spirit are given to each one to profit with. What gift has God given to you, and are you really profiting with it? If you are a Christian, I am certain that at least one of these gifts has been allocated to you, but it will not function effectively unless you walk in the Spirit. God has put the gift in you in order to be able to accomplish His purpose in the lives of others through you. If you are walking in the Spirit, the gift of the Spirit or the power of God will manifest through you to destroy the works of darkness (sin, sickness, poverty, and spiritual attacks) in the lives of people around you. We are vessels through which God seeks to manifest His will in this world. Walking in the Spirit enables us to affect and impact the lives of people around us. If there is no clear evidence of God walking through you to affect the lives of others, this may be an indication that you are not walking enough in the Spirit. God is therefore by this study calling you to a deeper and consistent walk in the Spirit.

LOVE AS EVIDENCE

Love is the second but ultimate evidence of walking in the Spirit. "But the fruit of the Spirit is love, joy, peace, longsuffering, gentleness, goodness, faith, meekness, temperance: against such there is no law" (Galatians 5:22–23). Just as a tree is identified by its fruit, so also the fruit of the Spirit reveals those who are walking in the Spirit. Note that it is the fruit, not fruits; it is only one fruit, and the summary is love. Remember that God is love, and if we are led by the Spirit or walk in the Spirit, we should manifest love. That is why the Bible says, "Beloved, let us love one another: for love is of God; and every one that loveth is born of God, and knoweth God. He that loveth not knoweth not God; for God is love" (1 John 4:7–8). "And we have known and believed the love that God hath to us. God is love; and he that dwelleth in love dwelleth in God, and God in him" (1 John 4:16). "We know that we have passed from death unto life, because we love the brethren. He that loveth not his brother abideth in death. Whosoever hateth his brother is a murderer: and ye know that no murderer hath eternal life abiding in him" (1 John 3:14–15). These passages speak for themselves. If you do not love, you do not know God, and God is not dwelling in you. Love is the proof that we have passed from death to life. A person without love is even referred to as a murderer, meaning that he or she has no part in the kingdom of God. "If I speak in the tongues of men and of angels, but have not love, I am only a resounding gong or a clanging cymbal. If I have the gift of prophecy and can fathom all mysteries and all knowledge, and if I have a faith that can move mountains, but have not love, I am nothing. If I give all I possess to the poor and surrender my body to the flames, but have not love, I gain nothing" (1 Corinthians 13:1–3). Without doubt, love is the ultimate evidence that we are in the Spirit and that we walk in the Spirit because God is love and the Spirit is God. "And we have known and believed the love that God hath to us. God is love; and he that dwelleth in love dwelleth in God, and God in him" (1 John 4:16). As Christians God dwells in us, but the circle will not be complete unless we dwell in Him also, and because He is love, we will also love when we dwell in Him. In fact, love is the evidence that we are disciples of Jesus, the confirmation that we are actually following Him. "A new commandment I give unto you, That ye love one another; as I have loved you, that ye also love one another. By this shall all men know that ye are my disciples, if ye have love one to another" (John 13:34–35). In the future, we shall consider love in detail, but in the meantime let us observe our actions closely; do they testify that we are walking in the Spirit? Because you cannot walk in the Spirit and fail to love. Love is the natural outcome when we walk in the Spirit, and we can say that he who walks in the Spirit walks in love.

SOUND MIND AS EVIDENCE

The third evidence that we are walking in the Spirit is a sound mind. As we have already seen, to walk in the Spirit is to be led by the Holy Spirit. Being led by the Spirit is really the ultimate that any human being should hope for because it implies good decisions and sound judgments, which translate to functioning in the wisdom of God. When you are led by the Spirit, the mind of Christ is being made available to you, and when you accept by walking in the Spirit, you deploy the mind of Christ. When you continuously walk in the Spirit in this manner, the mind of God becomes a part of you, and you can be said to have the mind of Christ. "For who hath known the mind of the Lord, that he may instruct him? but we have the mind of Christ" (1 Corinthians 2:16). The mind of Christ is actually the mind of God because He is the revelation of God to mankind (Hebrews 1:3). The Holy Spirit is the only one who has access to the deep things of God. "But as it is written, Eye hath not seen, nor ear heard, neither have entered into the heart of man, the things which God hath prepared for them that love him. But God hath revealed them unto us by his Spirit: for the Spirit searcheth all things, yea, the deep things of God. For what man knoweth the things of a man, save the spirit of man which is

74

in him? even so the things of God knoweth no man, but the Spirit of God" (1 Corinthians 2:9–11). Just as no one else knows your mind apart from your spirit, so also it is only the Holy Spirit who truly knows the mind of God. When we allow the Holy Spirit to lead us, we are actually allowing Him to search the heart of God to provide solution for our lives. That is why sound decisions and judgment are the result when we walk in the Spirit, and the more we respond to the leading of the Holy Spirit, the more our minds will be renewed and become sound, manifesting the mind of Christ. If you are not operating in soundness of mind, it means you are not walking in the Spirit, meaning you are not responding to the leading of the Holy Spirit. The major reason the Holy Spirit has been made to dwell in us is to lead us, and if you are not allowing Him to lead you, you are denying yourself the privileges and benefits of His ministry in your life. Walking in the Spirit helps to exercise your spiritual senses to produce a soundness of mind that is beyond the natural. "But strong meat belongeth to them that are of full age, even those who by reason of use have their senses exercised to discern both good and evil" (Hebrews 5:14).

CHAPTER 6

CONCLUSION/
FINAL THOUGHTS

ABIDING IN THE Spirit is the key to walking in the Spirit. The longer you abide or remain in the Spirit, the more you are able to walk in the Spirit. The key to abiding is fellowship. We have already learned how to walk in the Spirit, but if you really want to walk in the Spirit, you must learn to fellowship with the Holy Spirit. For effective fellowship with the Holy Spirit, you must also learn to put on the new man by deliberately and consciously denying yourself. "And that ye put on the new man, which after God is created in righteousness and true holiness" (Ephesians 4:24). As a child of God, you are a new creature; there is a new man or new nature in you that has been empowered to walk in the Spirit. This new man naturally dwells or lives in the Spirit. "But ye are not in the flesh, but in the Spirit, if so be that the Spirit of God dwell in you. Now if any man have not the Spirit of Christ, he is none of his" (Romans 8:9). To walk successfully in the Spirit, we must learn to separate the new man from the flesh. That is to say, you must know your flesh. If you do not learn to recognize your own flesh, you cannot effectively walk in the Spirit. The flesh, in every human being is not exactly the same though there are similarities. If you do not learn to recognize your own flesh, you will be deceived because you will confuse the voice of the flesh with the voice of the Spirit. The greatest danger that can befall a Christian is for the flesh to succeed in employing the power of the new man in its own service. The new man is not designed to be independent. The new man is successful only in union with the Holy Spirit. Outside the Holy Spirit the new man though may have developed in capacity is not effective in kingdom matters. The growth of the new man is to enhance or enlarge the activities of the Spirit in your life. It is dangerous to employ the power of the new man to serve the flesh; that is why we must walk in the Spirit. Two key words that can best describe walking in the Spirit are dependence and intimacy. If you learn to be dependent and intimate with the Holy Spirit, you will flow in the Spirit and have a proper Christian life with all the benefits. Don't try to be smarter than Jesus; He was completely dependent on the Spirit. He did nothing outside of the Spirit. Everything He did was by the Spirit. He is our example, and we must learn from Him. The reason many of us are unable to walk effectively in the Spirit is because we want to be independent in some areas of life. Complete dependence on the Holy Spirit is what we need to walk in the Spirit, and it is the only way we can survive the tricks of the Devil, the world, and the flesh. You cannot be dependent until you are intimate with the Holy Spirit. The more you are intimate, the more you will be able to depend on Him. The greatest asset a Christian can possess is intimacy with the Holy Spirit. This is what we ought to be laboring for. This is where we should focus all our energy because if we succeed in intimacy with the Holy Spirit, we will succeed as Christians and manifest Christianity as God designed it. This is what the anointing is all about. The Holy Spirit seeks intimacy with us; let us cooperate with Him. Intimacy with the Holy Spirit is possible only as we are full of the Spirit. You must desire to be full of the Spirit at all times. In fact, the Bible encourages continuous fullness. "And be not drunk with wine, wherein is excess; but be filled with the Spirit" (Ephesians 5:18). We must learn to maintain the fullness of the Spirit upon our lives, and this can be achieved only as we give priority to the things that keep us in His presence—continuous and conscious communication with the Holy Spirit, that is, speaking to the Spirit and hearing Him. In conclusion let me emphasize that walking in the Spirit will be impossible without total dependence on and intimacy with the Holy Spirit. Intimacy can never be achieved from a distance. You must come close to develop intimacy. In fact, God expects you not only to come closer but also to cling to Him. "Choose to love the Lord your God and to obey him and to cling to him, for he is your life and the length of your days. You will then be able to live safely in the land the Lord promised your ancestors, Abraham, Isaac, and Jacob" (Deuteronomy 30:20 LB). "Be sure to continue to obey all of the commandments Moses gave you. Love the Lord and follow his plan for your lives. Cling to him and serve him enthusiastically" (Joshua 22:5 LB). Though this is specifically referring to Israel, it is also applicable to us today. To successfully walk in the Spirit, we must be ready to cling to God and serve Him enthusiastically. "'Even as a loincloth clings to a man's loins, so I made Judah and Israel to cling to me,' says the Lord. 'They were my people, an honor to my name. But then they turned away'" (Jeremiah 13:11 LB). Like Israel we have been designed to cling to God and, more than that, to become one spirit with the Lord. "But he who is united to the Lord becomes one spirit with him" (1 Corinthians 6:17 RSV). We can say that by the new birth we have been made intimate with the Lord, but because we are not clinging to Him, intimacy is eluding us. In fact, not to be intimate after the new birth experience actually means that we are ignoring or turning away from the Lord. May you not be found guilty of ignoring the Lord, in Jesus's name. If you want to be successful in walking in the Spirit, dependence and intimacy with the Holy Spirit must become your priorities. You must work at it diligently day and night.

FINAL THOUGHT

Thank God that you were able to follow us to the end of this study. I am sure you can now agree with me that walking in the Spirit is critical to our success in the Christian race. I, therefore, use this opportunity to encourage you to put what you have read into practice. Don't forget that the truth practiced is the truth learned. If you do not immediately begin to practice the things you have learned, you will soon forget them. Walking in the Spirit is for your own benefit; it is the only way you can attain the fullness of God's plan for your life.

Don't forget that whatever is not of the Spirit is of the flesh. "That which is born of the flesh is flesh, and that which is born of the Spirit is spirit" (John 3:6 RSV), and whatever is not for God is for the Devil. "Likewise, my brethren, you have died to the law through the body of Christ, so that you may belong to another, to him who has been raised from the dead in order that we may bear fruit for God. While we were living in the flesh, our sinful passions, aroused by the law, were at work in our members to bear fruit for death. But now we are discharged from the law, dead to that which held us captive, so that we serve not under the old written code but in the new life of the Spirit" (Romans 7:4–6 RSV). The only way we can bear acceptable fruit for God is by walking in the Spirit. Practice, they say, makes perfect; you must begin to consciously practice walking in the Spirit in order to tap into the benefits of this message.

Finally, I believe God has spoken to you. I pray that you will be a doer, not a hearer only, and don't forget that to be a doer you must be diligent in looking and hearing. God is interested in seeing changes in our lives and in our relationship with Him. Let us not continue to take His patience for granted. "The Lord is not slack concerning his promise, as some men count slackness; but is longsuffering to us-ward, not willing that any should perish, but that all should come to repentance" (2 Peter 3:9). Let's put more effort into the things of the Spirit. We must become hungrier for the presence of God for our daily lives. Like King David we must thirst for God. "As the hart panteth after the water brooks, so panteth my soul after thee, O God. My soul thirsteth for God, for the living God: when shall I come and appear before God?" (Psalm 42:1–2). Immeasurable blessings await us as we give ourselves wholly to the Lord. Our labor in the Spirit will never be in vain. "Be not deceived; God is not mocked: for whatsoever a man soweth, that shall he also reap. For he that soweth to his flesh shall of the flesh reap corruption; but he that soweth to the Spirit shall of the Spirit reap life everlasting. And let us not be weary in well doing: for in due season we shall reap, if we faint not" (Galatians 6:7–9).

God bless you richly as you begin to redirect your efforts and time to those things that will enable you to walk smoothly in the Spirit.

CONTACT INFORMATION

REDEMPTION
PRESS

To order additional copies of this book, please visit
www.redemption-press.com.
Also available on Amazon.com and BarnesandNoble.com
Or by calling toll free 1 (844) 273-3336.

CPSIA information can be obtained at www.ICGtesting.com
Printed in the USA
LVOW12s0815080814

397921LV00001B/19/P

9 781632 324542